GET POOR NOW, AVOID THE RUSH

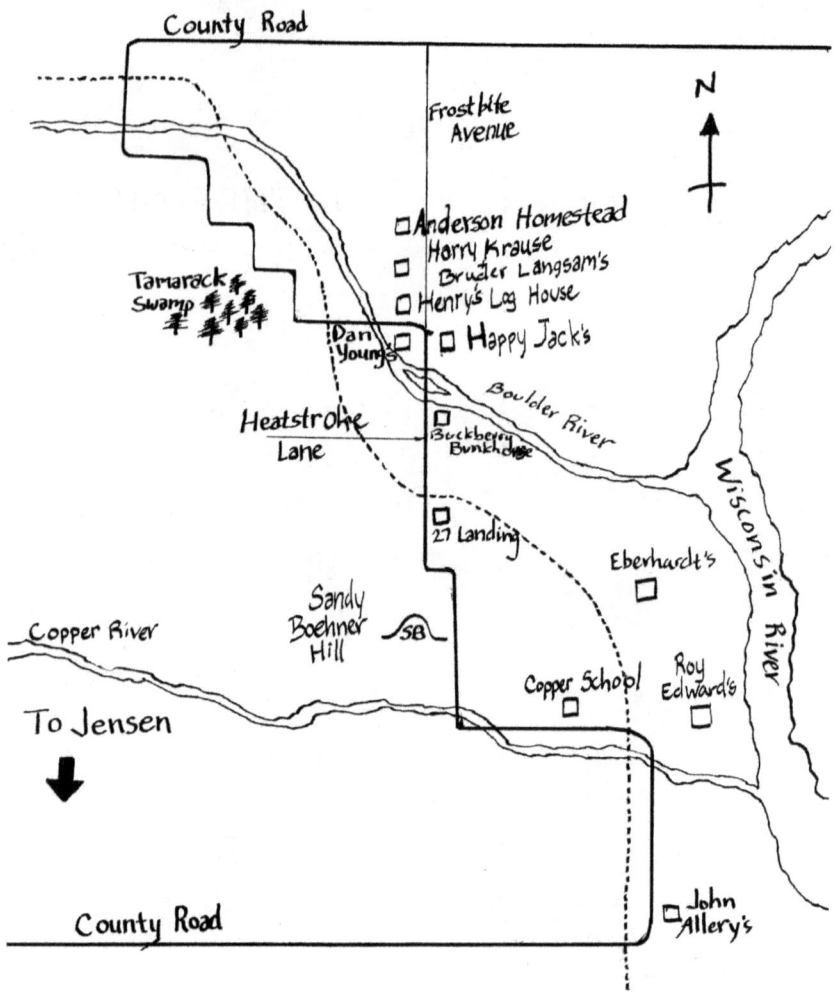

Get Poor Now, Avoid the Rush
The Life and Times of Henry Buckberry

by Seedy Buckberry

RESOURCE *Publications* • Eugene, Oregon

GET POOR NOW, AVOID THE RUSH
The Life and Times of Henry Buckberry

Copyright © 2011 Seedy Buckberry. All rights reserved. Except for brief quotations in critical publications or reviews, no part of this book may be reproduced in any manner without prior written permission from the publisher. Write: Permissions, Wipf and Stock Publishers, 199 W. 8th Ave., Suite 3, Eugene, OR 97401.

Resource Publications
An Imprint of Wipf and Stock Publishers
199 W. 8th Ave., Suite 3
Eugene, OR 97401

www.wipfandstock.com

ISBN 13: 978-1-60899-787-9

Manufactured in the U.S.A.

For Birdy

Whether I shall turn out to be the hero of my own life, or whether that station will be held by anybody else, these pages must show. To begin my life with the beginning of my life, I record that I was born. . . .

CHARLES DICKENS
David Copperfield, p. 13

Contents

Acknowledgments | ix

Introduction | xi

1 Dawson | 1

2 Jensen and Boulder | 22

3 Deadhead Poverty PhD | 41

4 Ends Too Short To Use | 61

5 Our Name Ain't Buckberry | 85

6 Depression Beehive | 112

7 Beaver, Deer, Fish, and Potatoes | 127

Afterword | 141

Acknowledgments

Thanks to Henry for wanting to do this, to Birdy for helping us get started, and to Sarah Blake for her virtuosity at the keyboard.

Finally, I should probably thank Paul Gilk for alerting me to Resource Publications. But, to tell the truth, I'm a little put out because he has apparently referred to me as "an elusive scarecrow of the northwoods" in his virtually unreadable *Polemics and Provocations*. It's hard, I confess, to be grateful to someone who's so snooty, condescending, and supercilious. I guess we all have a cross to bear. I just wish mine lived on the other side of the Wisconsin River.

Introduction

ON AN AFTERNOON IN September, 1987, I began a project that has languished—the recording of my father's stories, his life history. On that particular day—new moon, autumn equinox, cloudless high-pressure sunshine—we drove up a string of town roads, in my father's tan pickup, to Rutabaga Lake in the Porcupine Hills. Fishing. That was our excuse.

I brought along, for the very first time, a little battery-powered tape recorder I'd bought (for less than forty dollars) with the one-hundred dollar bill my older brother Albert had given me (shameless beggar) to get the project underway. I punched the "record" button.

"Maybe this machine won't work in the truck," I said.

"What?" my father yelled.

It was noisy, dust billowing up behind as we sped north.

I repeated what I'd said, then added, "Maybe we'll have to talk directly into the microphone."

"Oh, I imagine you'll have to talk right inta the mike," he replied. Mr. Professional.

It was obvious we were already practicing. Our voices had a self-conscious, artificial edge. Strictly amazing.

I paused and began pontificating into the electronic whirligig.

"Here it is the first day of fall," I said, "and we're headed toward a little lake to go fishing, my dad and I. We've got the little grey pram in the back of the pickup, the wind is blowin the leaves, most of the hardwoods have already turned color. The popples are just startin to turn. Some of the hardwoods, in fact, have their leaves down already.

"We're headed for a whole boat load of crappies, according to my father."

"What we haven't got room in the boat for," he butts in, "we got a fish stringer along ta tie'em on behind." He wasn't about to be left out of this Speaking On The Record. It was, after all, *his* life story we were supposed to be working on.

"The whole purpose of this tape recorder business is to get my father's stories and life history"—as if I hadn't already said this—"and I've been putting the project off for weeks and months and years because I don't know how to do it."

I paused there to fiddle with the machine. And to think of what to say next.

"I think we're after a book," I say, in a voice that invites my father to slip in a word or two. The machine is running smooth and slippery.

"Huh?" he says.

"I think we're after a book," I repeat more loudly.

"I don't know what you said." I know he's hard of hearing, but this is not quite getting off on the right foot.

"I - SAID - I - THINK - WE'RE - AFTER - A - BOOK!"

"We're goin after a *buck*?" he asks, throwing me a puzzled look. There's real confusion in his voice.

"A *BOOK*!" I shout, exasperated.

"A book of what?" he asks. There's not a hint of tease or guile in his voice.

"A book of *your stories*!" I reply. I can't quite believe this.

"A book of what?" he repeats.

"A book of YOUR STORIES!" I am yelling, but whether at him or at myself for dreaming up this hare-brained project is not clear.

"Ooooh," he says, "a book of 'your stories'!" Now he feels like we're getting somewhere. I resist a nearly overpowering impulse to throw the tape recorder in the ditch.

The confusion passes. That confusion does pass is one of life's blessings. My father starts to settle in. Sort of.

"Well, just turn that thing off. I need ta think a while. Don't waste yer film—ah, yer film, I mean yer tape. When I think a somethin then I'll, well . . . I might think a somethin yet, before the day's over. I usually do. My head's always full a that little garbage, ya know." He laughs. "I can't help it. That's the way I was born, I guess. Like they always usta say, 'Little head, little wit; big head, full a shit.'"

Our voices go "off the air" in laughter.

At that point I played back what we'd recorded, high volume, and we laughed over the conversation—though a little uneasily, too, hearing our voices, unfamiliar. Then I punched "record" again and got him going for a good half-hour. By that time we were in the Porcupine Hills. As we scooted around curves on the narrow gravel roads, through gorgeous deciduous forest, there were tears running down my father's face. Some deep memories were already coming up and out. By golly, I thought, this is going to be a whole lot easier and much better than I imagined.

We found our lake, got the pram in the water, and fished for several hours, meditating on bobbers floating in the unknown. In the twilight we quit, with exactly one small crappie and one tiny perch in a monstrous five-gallon bucket. The unknown had not been particularly generous.

My father drove us home. Neither of us had an interest in more story recording. It was pitch dark when I returned to my wood hut in the pine woods behind my father's house. I lit kerosene lamps (no electricity or running water for me) and backed the tape up, eager—very eager—to hear that last half-hour.

Of course I backed it up too far and heard again, with amused satisfaction, our initial confusion. And then, with great anticipation, nothing. Absolutely *nothing*. Just the dreadful sound of blank tape.

"Horseshit!" I hollered. I smacked the table with the flat of my hand, and the poor little tape recorder jumped in fear. "Don't hit me," it seemed to plead. "You're the idiot, not I."

That was nearly twenty years ago. On January 9, 2007, Otto Henry Buckberry will be ninety-five years old. I think it's time I punched some buttons right.

C. D. (Seedy) Buckberry
October 20, 2006

1

Dawson

WHEN I WENT UP to the ladies in the courthouse there in Steele, which is in Kidder County in south-central North Dakota, to see if I'd ever been born—I needed proof, see, so I could get on the good side a those Social Security people—and I told'em it had been awful cold that January night in 1912 when I was born in Dawson, one of 'em says, "And how do you know?" And I says right back to her, quick as a cat, "Well, I was *there*, so I guess I oughta know."

They got a laugh outa that.

My oldest sisters were Clara and Mary, goin up the ladder, so ta speak. I was the third child, see, the oldest boy, of what turned out ta be thirteen kids. I spoze you could call it a Baker's Dozen. But my Ma did all the bakin, and she did it all at home. In the oven and out. Her name was Gertrude.

My Pa's name was Otto. They were gonna give me his name as a middle name, see, but with Henry as a first name and Otto as a second and Buckberry draggin up the rear, that figured out ta be HOB.

Now what's a HOB? It ain't nothin but a countryman, a rustic, a clown, a hobnail, or somethin that juts out ta hang somethin on, like a *hob* in the back of a fireplace, somethin you can use ta hang a pot on. I looked it up in the dictionary once, when I was in the eighth grade in the Copper School, an just about ready ta graduate inta the world, ya might say. Figured I'd better know what a "hob" was before I left the dictionary for good.

And my Ma, she says—she was smart and kinda big and pretty quiet like, but sometimes she said things you didn't know quite how ta take—well, my Pa and Uncle Hugo were talkin about this HOB thing, sittin close to the cookstove, and my Ma, about ready ta pop with me inside, she says, kinda ta nobody in perticular, "Put you a 'O' on the end a HOB and you got yourself a nice little HOBO."

Now that was too much fer Pa. He was a small man, a jack a all trades ya might say, master a none, never really successful at ennything in perticular (except maybe makin babies), an maybe he sometimes took offence where none was intended.

So he sat there by the stove, stewin and smoulderin, chewin on somethin in the deep, dark stronghold of his mind, till he finally looks over at Ma, who was darnin a sock by the light of a kerosene lamp, an he says, "If it's a boy, an I hope it is, it's gonna be Otto Henry Buckberry. O. H. B. Now what kinda word you gonna wreck outa that, Gerty?"

People were into initials, I guess, more than now, took'em kinda serious, an Pa wasn't too keen a there always bein a HOBO at the table. So he stuck Otto up front, put Henry in the middle, just ta steer clear a me becomin a HOBO.

That never stopped my Ma from callin me her Little Hobo. But she never did it when Pa was around. It was a kind a tenderness between us. The last time I kin remember her callin me Little Hobo was when the family—almost all of'em, ennyway—was about ta get aboard the train in 1936 ta leave Wisconsin for the state a Washington.

It was almost twenty years before I saw her again. But I kin remember her lookin me in the eyes an sayin "Take care a yerself, Little Hobo," as if it was yesterday. An I remember turnin away with kinda watery eyes and a prickly sort a feelin up inside a my nose.

Ya, well, I cudda gone with'em, but I didn't. That was a hard moment. Almost changed my mind. As I had told Ma earlier, when she was beggin me ta come along, I sez ta her, "My little log shack's the best home I ever had, and I ain't chasin ennymore a Pa's dreams."

I kin remember she cried about that. Best not to dwell on it now. What good does that do?

Whether that HOBO name was good fer me I can't say, but I suspect it kind a softened up my point a view, for when the Great Depression spread an there were little hobos everywhere, I never thought ta look down on'em. I was one of 'em myself.

So they called me Henry, ennyway. You kin call me Hank. Most everybody does. But only my Ma got ta call me her Little Hobo. I ain't invitin you ta do it.

Maybe I got some a my Pa's thin skin, after all.

I'm gonna tell you my life's story—though I heard once about a old-timer an he was asked "You lived here all yer life?" an he shot right back, "Not yet."

So I'm gonna tell you my life's story, but it ain't done, yet. I got five and a half years ta go before my driver's license expires, an by then I'll be a hunnerd, an I don't believe in payin for somethin I don't get full use of. I'm kind of a tight old bugger.

It'd be nice ta hit one hunnerd. Ain't many people do. An I heard there ain't hardly ennybody dies *over* a hunnerd, so if a person makes it that far, he just might be home free. It's worth a try.

When I say I'm gonna tell you my life's story, I don't mean ta be braggin. I ain't nothin special, though I did live through interesting times—hard times, some of it, real hard.

When I say I'm gonna tell you my stories, you got ta know *it's the times* I want ta tell you about. *It's the times* what were so interesting. And if I get ta braggin a little, and I suspect I will, especially once we get to the deer huntin part, just look the other way a while an put up with it.

I'm an old man now, livin in my memories. As my son Seedy says—an it's him who's takin all this down—"You got to cut the Old Man some slack." He says that, sometimes, to his older brother Albert, when Birdy pushes in a little too hard.[1]

But maybe we best get started at the beginning. We ain't up to the wild north woods a Wisconsin yet. We ain't even up to the First World War. It's January of 1912 and a little squallin boy jest got himself born in

---

1. Albert became Bert, Bert became Berty, and Berty became Birdy. I guess Gramma's way with words got kind of stuck in the family. S. B.

a drafty frame house on the cold, windy prairie a Dawson, North Dakota, an got himself called Hank. O. H. B. Not a HOB but still a Little Hobo.

William H. Taft was President a the United States, and the last massacre a Sioux Indians—Big Foot and his folks—happened only twenty-two years earlier. Men still rode horses when I was a kid, a few packed side arms, and a fellow from Dawson—well, sort a from Dawson—got himself hung from the stockyard gate over in Steele,

I'll tell ya about that later.

Sometimes I think I'd a loved to have been there, in that "Old Wild West," and other times I'm damned glad I wasn't. It's a good thing we don't get to choose when we want ta be born. We'd be changin our minds all the doggone time.

I don't like teasin. Never did. An I don't like sayin I'm gonna do somethin *sometime* in order to get yer hopes up an then dangle that somethin like a worm on a hook. I've had it done ta me, an I plain don't like the feel of it.

So I'm gonna tell you about that hanged man, just ta get it outa the way, so ta speak. Sometimes you kin wait for somethin that, when it finally happens, wasn't worth waitin for. You decide for yerself whether this one wudda been worth the wait.

There was a middle-aged man in Dawson by the name a Tommy Glass. An he had a good-lookin daughter who got courted by a drifter, whose name I honestly can't recall. Ennyway, she married this drifter and they had a couple kids an then trouble set in an she went back ta live with her pa, with Tommy Glass.

One day that drifter came to the door, an when Tommy Glass opened up the drifter shot him dead, stepped over the body, went in an found his wife an shot her dead.

He tried ta get away with the two kids, but the town marshal got him and tied him up. The marshal took'em ta Steele. There wasn't enny jail in Dawson.

The ropes were hurtin, apparently, so the drifter said ta the marshal, "You tied me awful tight," and the marshal spozed ta have pulled his gun an said, "I kin fix yer pain right now, if that's what yer askin for."

So the marshal took that man ta jail in Steele, but the Dawson men had got themselves all worked up. An they took the law inta their own hands. If you study history, you'll see there were lots a vigilante men in the Old West, an this thing here in Steele mighta been near the tail end of it. They went ta the jail, several Dawson men, at night, in a buckboard pulled by a team a mules, overpowered the jailer, took that drifter man and hung him from the stockyard gate.

Now nobody talked about that in town. Nobody. At least not in the open. But Pa and Ma talked about it at home, an I was all ears.

See, there was a drayman in Dawson, an he had a pair a mules. His name was Larry Gazesky, an he made his livin by drayin—haulin stuff— for people. An the night a the hangin there was the sound of a team bein hitched to a buckboard, an that team had a pair a rattlin heel chains, an the only man in town who had heel chains on his team was Larry Gazesky.

Next mornin the news was all over town—nobody talked, everybody knew— there'd been a hangin in Steele. And my Pa, at breakfast, tryin, ya know, ta act like it was nothin out a the ordinary, said, "The buckboard's parked backwards from how I left it last night."

Larry Gazesky let it be known all over town that somebody had taken his mules without his knowledge or consent, but whether that was true or if he was coverin his tracks, I never knew, never asked, an nobody ever said.

An maybe the same kin be said a Pa an his buckboard.

I don't mean ta say that Pa was directly in on that vigilante hangin. He wasn't. That I wudda known about, sooner or later, one way or the other, eventually. But the buckboard thing, that's not clear. Was it stole? Was it asked for? Was it offered?

Those are some a the things nobody'll ever know. Not now ennyway. Not ennymore.

There was no such thing as blacktop on the roads when I was a kid. Not in Dawson. All dirt. An when it was wet, which wasn't too offen, it was a mess. An when it was dry, which was a lot, it was dust. That's just the way it was.

Everybody drove horses. There were very few cars, an none at all in the wintertime.

The main car was the Model T, an I kin remember the very first ride I ever got. It was a real thrill. A guy picked me up an gave me a ride home from school. That car had a cover on the top, ya know, from front ta back, an a couple rows a seats cobbled in ta sit on.

This particular car was fer haulin men. It was a old cripple of a car. But it ran.

The fella that drove the car usta haul duck hunters. There were lots a little lakes near Dawson. They called it The Land a the Potholes. You could go ennywhere an then all at once there was a slough, with rushes, or a little lake—an usually they were hooked up, one ta the other, somewheres.

An ducks. Man! Lots a ducks.

A man named Rhodes lived right close ta us, an he usta cater to the duck hunters. Him an his wife. They had a big house, an Mrs. Rhodes'd cook for those hunters.

She didn't have enny refrigeration, but out in their yard they had some little trees growin, an in under'em they had these little sheds, kinda like dog houses, but built up in the air, off the ground, with wire around'em. The hunters'd hang ducks in those little sheds, hang'em by the necks, an in the morning when Old Rhodes took the hunters out ta the potholes, with that other man (I can't remember his name, either), the one with the Model T, Mrs. Rhodes'd offen come ta our house draggin all the ducks she could handle.

Those ducks weren't spoilt yet, but the hunters always shot way more ducks than they could eat, an Mrs. Rhodes would bring'em ta Ma, just ta get rid of'em, otherwise they'd hang in those goofy dog houses and start ta stink.

Now those hunters had come ta Dawson on the train. Both freight and passenger came right through town. Those fellas came from the east, somewhere, an they only came in part ta shoot ducks. They also came ta drink.

Now Dakota was dry, strictly dry. But these men had their booze with'em, an at night they'd drink an play cards, an in the mornin Old Rhodes'd take'em back out to the potholes ta shoot more ducks.

Those guys jest came out ta drink an shoot. They didn't have a thought about savin nothin. They jest shot. An Mrs. Rhodes'd drag ducks over ta Ma. We ate lotsa ducks.

One a those hunters had a servant, or a valet, or whatever ya call'em, an he was a black man. He was the first black man I ever saw.

Besides bringin Ma ducks, Mrs. Rhodes also bought milk an cream an butter from Ma. We had eight or ten cows. An, so, one day this black man came over after milk. An he was a nice man—dressed up good, an all that. An my Pa's Pa had killed a badger, an my Pa had skinned it.

Grampa's dog, name a Caesar, had got ta fight with that badger—that's the story my Pa told, ennyway—an the badger was lickin the dog, so Grampa killed the badger with a stick. An he showed it to my Pa, an Pa skinned it. Did a good job a doin it, too. Looked good.

So when that black man saw the hide, he wanted it. Wanted that badger skin. An my Pa sold it to'em for two dollars.

Pa laughed about it, thought it was a big joke. Sold a worthless badger skin to a black man for two dollars.

But it was a nice hide. I liked it, too. I never did understand what was so funny about that black man wantin that badger skin.

If I'd had two dollars, I wudda bought it myself.

I always had a funny feelin about my Pa's laughin over that badger skin an the black man who bought it fer two dollars. Still puzzles me.

I'll tell ya more about badgers later. Can't get *everything* in at once.

Frost last night. September ninth ain't bad fer here. I got corn froze off once on the Fourth a July. That hurt.

I know you ain't gonna be back fer lunch, Seedy. I kin make my own. Two, three, four, five eggs or so. I like'em.

Reminds me. My Ma's Pa, Grampa Coster, came out ta North Dakota from Kentucky once, I don't know what for, an he woke me early in the mornin, before ennybody else was up, an he took me by the hand an outside an all around the house, an damned if we didn't find two nests with Easter eggs in'em.

Now my Ma had chickens, but those eggs were never colored like these were. I'd never heard a "Easter eggs" before, but my Grampa liked that sort a thing. In fact he told me, an I kin remember this like it was yesterday, that some fella he knew had eaten twenty-three a those "Easter eggs." That's a lot a eggs. I think he might've sprouted a whole flock a feathers.

Ya, Grampa was inta that "Easter egg" stuff. But he was like that. If he had it in his mind ta do somethin, well, he jest went an did it.

I remember when we were livin out here, by the Boulder River, in Wisconsin, an him an Gramma came out from town with one horse an a top buggy. This wudda been sometime in the middle nineteen-twenties. Gramma stayed with Ma, but Grampa took me, an I was just a kid, an we took all those back dirt roads over ta Chris Larsen's place, who lived near where the cranberry marsh is now.

I knew Chris Larsen because I went to the Copper School with a couple a Chris Larsen's kids. An everybody knew Chris Larsen cooked booze. Everybody knew it.

If there was a house party ennywhere in the neighborhood, Chris Larsen'd be there. The kids'd go inside and dance. Put records on the Victrola. Dance with the women. But not the men. They'd always be outside. We could hear'em talk and laugh, louder, ya know, as the party got goin. An Chris Larsen was always out there with'em.

Now Old Pete Peterson an his wife Mabel came ta one a these house parties. They lived on the east side a the Wisconsin River, but they came acrost in a old wooden rowboat. An when they were ready ta go home, Old Pete was so drunk Mabel wouldn't let him get in the rowboat with her. She got in, pushed him back, an rowed off without him.

But Harry Eberhardt had a leaky old skow pulled up on the bank there, an Old Pete flopped that skow upside down somehow, drug it in the water, laid on top, an paddled himself across the river with his hands.

People laughed about that for a long time after.

So I guided my Grampa over ta Chris Larsen's place, an when we got there—Chris Larsen didn't know my Grampa from Adam—I went right up ta Chris Larsen an sez to'em, "Grampa'd like some moonshine."

I could tell Chris was hesitant, actin almost like he didn't hear me or if I'd said somethin he didn't understand. But I just waited an perty soon Chris ambled off an before long he came back with a quart jar filled ta the brim. Had a lid on, a course. Two dollars, if I remember right.

An then back on all those dirt roads to our place ta get Gramma, an then they went back ta town. I'd a hated to be that horse that day. Probably close ta thirty miles for a stupid quart a booze. An I doubt if Grampa ever thought ta give that horse a shot a moonshine, ta thank'em for all that useless pullin.

I know I said I was gonna start at the beginnin a this story, in downtown Dawson, so ta speak, an I kin see that's what you'd like ta see happen, Seedy, but that ain't the way my mind works.

I'm ninety-four years old, goin on ninety-five, an if my mind wants ta go somewheres, then, by god, it's gonna go there. The reins are slack, if ya know what I mean. The horse's got the bit in his teeth.

This horse is retired, out ta pasture, an there ain't much gonna coax him inta a harness ever again. Now he's still wantin the feed bag an a water pail an a good snug stall, but the real life he's got is up in his head, all crowded with memories, an there's still some frisky colts in that corral, an they jest might go to buckin or prancin as the mood takes'em.

I'm jest along fer the ride. I ain't callin the shots. I'm jest describin the scenery.

So when you drove me ta town this mornin, an we went past the county gravel pit, down by the Boulder, an I saw how they're crushin up the last of it, startin already ta landscape the edges, figgerin, I suppose, ta shut it down perty soon, empty as a dead horse, maybe in a year or so, I started to remember how Oscar Weaver an me opened that pit in 1931.

I *think* it was 1931. I ain't under oath here, an I ain't testifyin in a court a law. *Maybe* it was 1931.

Ennyway, Oscar was a few years older'n me, an he had himself a single-axle truck with a little box on the back, good, maybe, for three-quarters of a yard a gravel, if ya heaped it up, an the town paid me a dollar a day ta be Oscar's shovelman.

The county road was almost brand new, all dirt, no gravel, an when it rained the dust turned ta mud and potholes in no time flat. Oscar, who also had a team a horses an some old derelict pony grader, was the town's patrolman, an he was supposed ta make a road outa that mess. An he had that truck. An he had me.

Well, at first he had another young fella ta help with the shovelin. The truck had ta be loaded by hand, see. Oscar had got himself, I don't know where, two big pieces a metal from a railroad car, an he laid them down end ta end at the base a the bank, an he'd back his truck onta those plates smack up against the bank, so the loadin was perty easy, an then he could drive off without gettin stuck.

This other young fella, his name was Eber Lansbach, he lasted one day. A dollar a day wasn't enough, he said, fer work that hard. An then Oscar went ta Old Man Karban who lived in a shack acrost the road from the pit. But Old Man Karban was maybe in his sixties already, divorced, with a couple a grown kids, had maybe a little savings, I don't know, an he supposedly told Oscar the same thing Eber had—too hard a work fer too little pay.

That's when Oscar came fer me.

Well, a dollar a day *wasn't* much money for that kind a work, even then, but I was young an big an strong, an I didn't have ennything else ta do, at least nothin that earned me enny money. Besides, Oscar had a single-shot twenty gauge shotgun that he carried in the cab, an it was my job ta shoot partridges out the window as we were takin a load out or comin back empty.

An that was right up my alley, though there wasn't enny front sight on that gun an I missed more than I hit, until I sez to Oscar, "You gotta put a sight on this gun. I'm missin too many birds, an I'm wastin yer shells."

Now Oscar kept all the birds I shot. All of'em I say. I never got a one. But he did get a sight glued on that gun an my aim did improve, an there were lots a partridges right out on the road, or close to it, and, man, I shot birds.

Now one day we were loadin gravel an a car stops on the road an out steps Leo Gould. Everybody knew Leo Gould. He was a tall, rangy man, an he was some sort a state fire warden, an before that he'd been a timber cruiser for the Kinzel Lumber Company. But as a fire warden he was also a game warden.

When Oscar saw who it was, he dropped his shovel real quick and walked fast ta the road. I kept shovellin, ya know, one eye on the gravel and three on Leo Gould, if ya know what I mean. Mostly I was wonderin, if Leo took a notion ta walk over to the truck with Oscar, how was I gonna get that shotgun out a the cab without bein seen, without gettin caught. There were three, four birds layin behind the seat.

All I know is, Leo didn't come back with Oscar, but, though he never said a word a why, Oscar never again brought that shotgun ta work with him in the truck. Which really took the fun out a loadin and haulin gravel, I'll tell you.

Those game wardens were *bad* men. They could really spoil a good time an make a mess outa things. You never wanted ta run acrost'em if you had somethin ta hide. I almost got caught once, but that's another story, an I ain't gonna tell it now.

But it sure is somethin. All those years fishin an trappin an huntin an I never once got pinched. Except fer the time the game warden fined me seventy-four dollars cuz you kids didn't have the right kind a life preservers on when we were in that rowboat fishin up on that backwater a the Wisconsin River. That doesn't count. That doesn't count at all. That was downright stupid. That game warden should a been ashamed of himself.

You kin laugh about it all you want, Seedy, but seventy-four dollars ain't nothing ta sneeze at.

I'm gonna tell ya two stories fer the price a one.

Two times nothin is still nothin, so don't be gettin yer hopes up.

When we were still in Dawson, my Ma always kept chickens, and a couple a times she tried turkeys. One year she went big an got herself about seventy-five baby turkeys, figgerin, ya know, to butcher'em in the fall and make herself some pocket money.

Those turkeys did real well, grew fast, grew big, loved ta eat grasshoppers, an there were grasshoppers everywhere. Problem was there were too many grasshoppers.

Well, that wudda been alright fer the turkeys, right up their alley, in fact, but butted up against our little place in Dawson was somebody's wheat field. An in that field grasshoppers were doin serious damage.

One day two men showed up with a team a horses and a buckboard and commenced ta drive back and forth through that field, one man drivin the team an the other broadcastin somethin out of a barrel.

Lookin back, we should a put all those turkeys in the barn, but we didn't. Nobody thought that the grasshoppers would eat the poison and, with the wind behind'em, fly just far enough ta drop dead in our yard. Easy pickins for seventy-five hungry turkeys.

It was like a battlefield, a turkey cemetery. Dead turkeys everywhere, a total loss.

Except fer one old tom who was fasting that day or was jest too tough ta die. Ma was sick at heart.

Another time my Pa was gone somewhere an I knew I shouldn't do it, but I jest had ta try out some a his carpenter tools. He had a set a wood augers—like a drill bit, ya know, mounted in a sturdy wooden handle, the whole thing shaped like a giant T. An I borrowed one of'em.

Well, first thing I found out was that I wasn't strong enuff ta drill a hole in the barn wall. So I looked for somethin I *could* make a hole in. Didn't take long ta discover that I could drill perty fine holes in the dirt, holes all over the yard, five, six, seven inches deep, maybe, the whole yard jest pocked with'em.

But after a while, ya know, it ain't very interestin enny more. Ya git tired a holes. So I put the auger away. That was in the afternoon. Found somethin else ta do.

In the evenin Ma calls ta me. She's kinda frantic cuz all the baby chicks are missin. "Come help me find the chickens," she sez, an so we go lookin everywhere in the barn with no luck at all. Then she sort a stumbles on one a them auger holes in the dirt, an down at the bottom a that hole there's two baby chicks, one on top a the other.

Turns out that everyone a those baby chicks had found a hole ta fall into, an we rescued every single one of'em alive. Ma was mad, but she was happy, too. So she let me off with only a hard scoldin, but, so far as I ever knew, she never told Pa.

I think I wudda got a lickin for sure.

I can't remember if I started school when I was five or when I was six. There wasn't enny such thing as kindergarden or—what do ya call it now? Pre-school. None a that. With my birthday in January, I probably started first grade when I was six.

First an second grade were in the same room. One teacher. Her name was Minnie Coulter. An us first graders got picture books with words under the pictures.

When I started, I couldn't read or write my own name, but I liked ta have that book, even asked ta take it home with me, an it fascinated me so much I damn near ate it. Wasn't long an I could read what it said under those pictures, an then I noticed that the first grade was broken up inta two groups, A and B, and I was in B.

By payin attention, I soon decided I could read jest as good as them in A, an so one mornin I went up ta Minnie Coulter an I told her I could read that book jest as good as the kids in A. So she sez, "You can? That's good. Go take your seat, Henry." So I took my seat, way in the back, acrost the aisle from a girl named Margaret Lunner. Everybody called'er Peggy.

An pretty soon Minnie Coulter calls the class to order, an then she calls me up front. She sez ta the class, "Henry will read to us now from our reading book. Just start at the beginning, Henry. I will tell you when to stop."

Well, my knees were knockin. I didn't expect that, at all, ta be told ta read ta the entire class. But what was there ta do but open that book an give it a try?

At first I was stutterin perty bad, but I soon got the hang of it an jest kept readin till Minnie Coulter sez, "Thank you, Henry. You may take your seat."

I guess I must a done okay, cuz from that day on I was no longer in B. I got ta be in A.

Now I kept that same seat, way in the back, an Peggy Lunner kept hers, all the while I was in school in Dawson. An she kind a got ta be my girlfriend—in school, I mean. At recess boys were with the boys an the girls were with the girls, an we didn't pay much attention to each other. But inside we were friends.

Peggy was good at reading, but she had a awful time with arithmetic, specially when we got ta long division. I liked it, even got kinda good at it, but Peggy, she was lost. Long division had her stumped.

It was that long division, maybe, that did it. Got'er ta be my girlfriend, I mean. Cuz when Minnie Coulter wasn't lookin, I'd hand Peggy my tablet, an she'd copy it all down.

I suspect Minnie Coulter knew what we were doin, but she had first grade and second grade, an then they gave her third grade besides, an that's a lot a kids. If I was helpin Peggy Lunner, that meant Minnie Coulter didn't have to. An maybe that's why she never said ennything. Maybe she was grateful.

The Northern Pacific Railroad came right through Dawson, freight plus one passenger train a day. There was a water tank an a coal docks, an some a those trains took on water an some took on coal an some took on both.

How my Pa got ta be friends with one a the engineers I do not know. But one day he took me by the hand and we walked down to the coal docks. A train was sittin there, loadin up, and the engineer was up in his seat, arm an head leaning out the little window. Pa was talking to'em, lookin up, talkin about things that don't mean ennything to a kid. I had my eyes on that big, black engine—huge steel wheels, drive shaft, jest the sheer massiveness a that monstrous big machine.

The engineer musta noticed how I was standin there, mouth hangin open, eyes as big as dinner plates, and he reached up a hand an twitched one a his controls. That train may a been jest sittin there, but it had a head a live steam, an when the engineer twitched that little lever, those huge wheels gave a lurch, like a dog havin a dream, an I about crapped my pants.

I looked up at'em an he jest grinned down at me. "Maybe you'll get to drive one a these someday," he sez, an he patted the outside metal like it mighta been a horse's neck. "When yer a little older, maybe yer Pa'll buy ya one."

They both got a big laugh out a that. I was too young ta know what was so funny. Though for a long time afterwards, I dreamt about gettin a train for my birthday. It had a mane a long hair runnin full-length down the roof a the cab, an instead of a whistle, it would whinny like a wild horse. I called it the Dakota Hobo.

It was probably 1918 or '19, an I was probably in the first grade, an the whole school was told that President Wilson's train'd be stoppin in Dawson, on such an such a day, an that we'd all get out a school ta go down to the water tank, an that the President would get out on the little platform on the back a the caboose an make a little speech.

I think the First World War was over by then becuz we were also told there'd be airplanes ta see that day, an nobody'd ever seen a airplane. So everybody got excited.

When that day came, we all got out a school, jest like we'd been told, all together in classes, ya know, an we walked on down to the water tank an got bunched together, an there we stood waitin for President Wilson's train. Bein antzy, ya know, the way kids are gonna be when they're jest standin around doin nothin, waitin for somethin ta happen.

An finally somebody sez, "I kin see it coming!" An, sure enough, perty soon we all kin see that train headed west acrost the prairie, smoke pourin out a the smokestack, an the ground startin ta tremble. An then we *really* started ta get excited! Here comes the President!

Well, all we got a President Wilson that day was a steam whistle, cuz that train never even slowed down fer Dawson, much less fer water at the tank. It jest flashed right on through.

We were awful disappointed. Had ta go back ta school.

But we weren't in the classroom long an somebody shouted "Airplanes!" I don't think ennybody waited fer Minnie Coulter ta say we could git up an go cuz we jest got up an went.

I suppose those planes—there were two of'em—were spozed ta arrive, ya know, when the President's train was taking on water, an make a really special show a the President's stop, but that train was long gone. So those airplane guys did their little loop-de-loops fer five, six minutes—double-winged outfits, ya know, with open cockpits—an some acrobatics, an then they turned and chased after Wilson's train. We stood an watched'em till they were out a sight with a funny kind a emptiness ya get when ya think, "That's the last time I'll ever see ennything like that." Those were the first airplanes I ever saw. An that's as close as I ever got to a President a these United States.

See, my Pa and Ma owned two, three acres on the south side a Dawson. A house, a barn, maybe eight or ten cows, an two teams a horses, one of which was all white. Pa called'em Shorty and Bell.

There was always a flock a chickens, sometimes a few turkeys, and in the spring, when Pa'd help a sheep rancher shear sheep—he'd be gone for a week or ten days—he'd come back with a lamb, usually, and we'd raise it up till fall, when Pa'd butcher it.

There ain't much meat on a sheep. They're all wool. But Pa liked his mutton.

Makes me think of a stupid little rhyme us kids'd recite ta each other—

> Mary had a little lamb,
> Her daddy killed it dead.
> Now she carries it ta school
> Between two hunks a bread.

At first my sister Mary thought it kinda funny. Then it made her mad.

Ennyway, Pa rented land near where Grandpa Buckberry lived, which was maybe a couple a miles south a town, an on that rented land he raised wheat. He made hay from a slough on the south side a Lake Isabel, all cut with a hand scythe, a course, an it was stacked in the open, my Ma up on the stack, an Pa hoistin the dried hay up ta her by means of a rig called a hay stacker.

Ma helped with the wheat harvest, too. Pa drove a three-wheeled contraption called a header, powered by two teams a horses *pushin* from behind, that cut the wheat off high and carried it on a canvas elevator an dumped it in a header wagon that Ma drove right alongside. When Ma's wagon was full, Pa'd stop, and she'd drive her team over to the wheat stack, where the wheat was heaped until the threshing machine came around.

It was real interestin to a kid. Sometimes I even got ta drive Ma's team.

Beyond Grampa's by a couple a miles was my Uncle Hugo's farm. I liked Uncle Hugo. He had two daughters and a son—Pauline, Mable, and John, all older'n me—and sometimes, fer no reason at all, Uncle Hugo'd give me a quarter.

A quarter was a lot a money to a little kid. I practically worshipped that man.

But him an my Pa didn't get on too good. Uncle Hugo was a hard-workin farmer, an my Pa was, well, nine o'clock was early enuff ta git started, an three o'clock was soon enuff ta quit. An so they didn't see eye ta eye.

I ain't sure what year it was, 1921 probably, when Pa sold the house and barn and the two, three acres there in Dawson, and we moved out ta Grampa's and built us a shack.

There was restlessness in the air those days. We never wintered in that shack.

Well, for the grownups there was restlessness. Not for me. I had ta herd cows all summer long. In the mornin I'd get up on one a Pa's old horses, bareback, an take the cows out ta pasture an stick with'em all day long. There ain't a lot a restlessness in that, exactly. Boredom maybe, but not restlessness.

But a kid kin only sit atop a old horse for so long, while cows are eatin or layin down an chewin their cuds, an pretty soon ya gotta get off that horse an walk around, stretch yer legs a little. An then you got yerself a problem.

It's easy enuff ta slide down from a big horse's back, but how do ya git back up? Ain't ennything ta climb up on out there on the prairie. No rocks, no stumps, no fence posts, no trees. Nothin.

Well, desperation is kind of a interestin teacher. I figured out that I could throw a leg over the horse's neck when she had her head down eatin, an when I did that she'd throw her head up quick an I'd go slidin down her neck to her back. Only I always did that facin her butt, so once I got on'er back, I'd have ta turn myself around in order ta be facin the right direction. I soon learned that a horse's mane is fer hangin onto.

But she was a slow, patient old plug, an we always got the job done.

In the evenings, the four of us oldest kids—Mary, Clara, me, and my next sister Daisy—had ta ride the horses, all four of 'em, to the lake ta water 'em. Clara was usually the fastest, an she'd grab the swayback mare an off she'd go, with the rest of us streakin along behind in her dust, all of us whoopin and bareback. There weren't enny saddles for us kids.

My cousin John had a pony an a saddle, an he'd come by ta play ball with us kids, but he never let me ride.

An when we lived in Dawson, a boy named Lloyd Rowland had a pony but no saddle, an once he came over when the folks were gone an we figgered out a way ta tie a long rope onta his pony's tail an hook it up to the handle of the new red wagon Pa'd bought fer me.

I rode in that wagon and Lloyd went gallopin down the street with me in the wagon, bouncin along behind, the rope tied to his pony's tail.

We got turned around alright, an when we came gallopin back to our place he turned into our driveway, but the wagon, with me in it, took a shortcut and rammed into a piece of wall, an a front wheel bent under the wagon box like a broken foot, an I went sprawlin in the dirt.

Though he fixed it for me, Pa gave me a lickin for the broken wheel, that bent axle, an Lloyd Rowland'n me never tried that trick again.

That restlessness in the air got stirred real good when my Ma's Pa came out ta visit from Ohio or Kentucky or wherever it was he lived. Grampa

Coster rented a house on the north end a Lake Isabel, an he lived there with Gramma and their daughter Minnie, who was my Ma's little sister. Who wasn't so little ennymore. She wanted a boyfriend, an maybe there wasn't one ta be found in Dawson. Or one she liked. I don't know. I was just a kid.

Grampa and Gramma and Minnie had been ta North Dakota once before. He was retired from bein a railroad mechanic, an he didn't like the smoky air of those factory towns. He liked the fresh, open air of Dakota.

When they had come in '17 or '18, they took a farm (I don't know if they bought it or jest rented) called the Fritz Place, a house an stable, jest beyond Uncle Hugo's. Grampa was gonna farm, raise wheat, an he bought a team a real good horses, got some plowin done, but one day a big Dakota storm rolled in, an when it rolled out one a Grampa's mighty fine horses was layin dead from a lightning strike.

He sold the other horse to the U.S. goverment, which was buyin horses for the war.

One time we'd come out from Dawson in Pa's buckboard, an Grampa was gone when we arrived. Perty soon he showed up with his slide action shotgun, all loaded down with wild game, about all he could carry. He had a string a ducks, a goose, an a jackrabbit, an he was the happiest man in the world.

Maybe if it hadn't been for Minnie Coster, the Buckberrys might a never left Dakota. I'm guessin, but I do wonder.

But in 1921, my Pa and Grampa Coster got their heads together, put on their suits, an took the train toward Fargo, inta the Red River Valley, an there was a lot a excited talk about maybe they were gonna buy a farm.

It was lots a years later that I learned that a lot a those "Bonanza" wheat farms in the Red River Valley—big ones, some of 'em hundreds a thousands of acres—had gone broke when wheat prices fell through the floor after the sky high prices of the First World War, an I think Pa an Grampa Coster thought they were gonna get a piece a prime wheat land on the cheap.

But they came back, after a week or so, an there wasn't much said, an that excitement just fizzled away.

But Minnie was itchin fer something better than the bare, open prairie a Dawson, North Dakota, an somebody—it might even a been my

Ma—heard there was lots a work in the lumber mills a Jensen, Wisconsin. It was probably somethin she'd read in a newspaper.

Since Grampa Coster had worked on the railroad, he had savings or a pension, I don't know which, but him an Gramma wanted Minnie ta stay close to'em, so Grampa an Minnie got on the train and went ta take a look at Jensen.

Gramma stayed with us. An perty soon Ma got a letter—Gramma couldn't read or write her own name—that Grampa and Minnie had found a big brick house on the southwest edge a Jensen, with maybe seventeen acres, an a crick runnin through, an he bought it.

So Ma packed Gramma on the train, an Jensen was the new place ta git excited about. I was excited, too. Excitement is kind a contagious, ya know. It's sort a like a disease.

We left Dawson for Wisconsin in October a 1921. So it must a been in the summer, or maybe early in September, that I found a very interesting rock on the shore a Lake Isabel, which is right near Dawson.

I took that rock ta school an showed it to Minnie Coulter. Her Ma had been midwife when I was born, so we had a special kind of attachment.

When Minnie Coulter examined that rock, she took me and the rock up ta see the lady who was principal of the school. That principal was tall and slender, with greying hair drawed back in a bun, and she hardly ever cracked a smile. She had those funny little glasses that perch on the nose, old-fashioned glasses that didn't have enny bows ta hook behind the ears, and there was a thin chain from the glasses to a pin on her jacket. Very dignified. Nobody ever sassed the principal or talked back to her. Nobody.

I knew that rock was an agate. But ta me it was only an interesting rock, a novelty. But the principal lady took that rock, stuck her glasses up on her nose, and *studied* that rock fer several minutes. I jest stood there watchin and waitin, real quiet.

When she was done *studyin* that rock, she took her glasses off, turned in her chair, and jest looked at me. She didn't hand the rock back ta me but set it real deliberate like at the side of her desk. Everything about her was real deliberate. I jest stood there waitin fer her ta say somethin.

"Henry," she finally says, "I would like to give you thirty-five cents for this agate. Will you sell it to me?"

Well, even if I'd wanted ta keep it, I probably couldn't a said no. Not to that scary lady with the funny glasses perched on her nose. I didn't have thirty-five cents, but I knew *exactly* what thirty-five cents would buy me. An I didn't waste enny time saying yes.

That thirty-five cents never made it home. At the hardware store in town, they sold gopher traps. Twenty cents each or two fer thirty-five. When I got home, I was carryin two gopher traps.

Ma had told me that there was a bounty on gophers. You bring in a hunnerd gopher tails an somebody'd pay you five dollars. Now five dollars seemed like a fortune ta me, an all of a sudden, on account a that agate, I had a way ta tap inta that fortune.

An did I trap gophers! I had a big collection a tails, but I was still short a one hunnerd when we got on that steam train, in Dawson, in October a 1921, an headed east acrost Minnesota an on into the scary woods of northern Wisconsin.

I never did get me that five bucks.

The folks got me a new suit a clothes for that train trip to Wisconsin, knee pants an a pair a ankle-high shoes. I'd never had ennything like that before.

In the summertime, in Dawson, us kids were always barefoot, jest as we would be again out in the Town a Boulder. But now, for the train, we were dressed neat and perty.

I'd never been on a train before, either. Seen lots of 'em—every day, perty much. But it was a big thrill ta actually get inside a one an sit on one a these big seats, though we didn't go jumpin around or runnin all over the place, the way kids do nowadays. Pa an Ma were strict, an we listened. We had ta mind.

We sat there an watched the prairie as it hurried away ta the west. At least that's how it seemed after a while. Yer sittin there half drowsy, kinda jiggled ta sleep by the rockin of the train, an it seems like you ain't the one that's movin but the land is. Gives you a kind a funny feeling, like the world's gone crazy.

We changed trains in Minneapolis or St. Paul, I don't remember which, an took the Soo Line inta Wisconsin all the way ta Heafford Junction. That train came to a complete stop on a low bridge over a lake—maybe it was a backwater of the Wisconsin River—an by then I wasn't sittin quite so tight in my seat ennymore, an I remember lookin out one window on one side, an then out the window on the other, an wonderin, scared like, why is this train standin on the water?

In Heafford Junction we changed trains again and came right on down the Milwaukee Road ta Jensen. From Tomahawk there was dense forest, trees makin the sides of a tunnel we were passin through, an I wasn't used ta that. I only knew about prairie, an potholes, an grassy sloughs. I didn't know ennything about forest. All I could think of was bears, the woods must be full of 'em, an it made me scared.

But I will say one thing that gave me confidence, whenever I put my hand in my pocket. While herdin Pa's cows the summer before, I'd come acrost a small heap a old boards jest layin out there on the prairie. An somewhere I found a wheel. So I borrowed some a Pa's tools an took'em with me on that old plug of a horse when I went out ta babysit those cows. An over two, three, four days, I made myself a little wheelbarrow.

For a kid it was a perty good job, if I do say so myself. But, of course, I couldn't bring it along ta Wisconsin. That was outa the question. So I sold it to a kid for fifty cents.

I hadn't made that five bucks for a hunnerd gopher tails, but I did have fifty cents for my little wheelbarrow.

I had two quarters in my pocket, so I didn't come ta Wisconsin broke.

2

Jensen and Boulder

When we came ta Wisconsin, ta Jensen, in October a '21, an we lived for a few months with Grampa an Gramma Coster in their big brick house, us kids what were old enough went to the Catholic school.

It musta been about a mile. We had ta walk up South Foster Street ta Main, then east on Main over the two big wooden bridges that crossed the Wisconsin River—the land between is nothin but a big, low island—an on east an north to the school.

Those big wooden bridges scared me cuz there'd be teams a horses pullin wagonloads a slabwood from the lumber mills—people burned wood, ya know, an everybody had a cookstove—an those horses would clomp, clomp, clomp on those wooden planks, an that whole bridge'd kinda tremble and jiggle.

East a those bridges there was a grocery store, on the corner of Prospect and Main, called Kohlhoff and Kreuger, and out on the sidewalk they had a wooden barrel full a long, split, dried fish, so tall that the tails were up above the rim. An we usta get a good laugh nearly every time we walked by.

There were dogs all over the place, see, an dogs are territorial critters. So one a the places the male dogs stopped ta make their presence known was that fish barrel, where they'd come ta lift their legs. We kids thought it was awful funny for those dried fish ta be gettin an extra dose a dog brine. That wasn't enny fish we were eager ta eat.

I usta follow some a the bigger boys ta school, an sometimes they'd take a shortcut acrost the railroad trestle an think nothin of it. But I was scared a bein up over the water like that an had ta step real careful on each and every tie, an those boys'd be long gone by the time I got acrost.

A couple a times in the winter I followed'em home, an they jest walked acrost the river ice, an that was scary, too. But I made it. They didn't pay much attention ta me. I was the new kid, jest nobody.

There was one boy, though, that paid attention ta me, an his name was John Ament. He was in my grade, a small kid, an we'd offen walk home together, cuz he lived somewhere near my Grampa's, though I was never in his house.

Ennyway, John Ament had a dog, a long-haired mutt, an in the winter—this happened lots a times—that dog'd meet John between the bridges, on our way home from school, an that dog had a little harness an was pullin a coaster sled. John an that dog'd run ta meet each other like long lost friends, an John'd spin that sled around, dive onta it belly first, an that dog'd take off for home with John ridin and laughin along behind.

I never did get a turn on that sled.

But there was a girl that liked me, too. Seemed like she took every chance there was ta be close ta me. At school, I mean. That's the only place I saw her. Her name was Catherine Bosworth.

When we moved out to the Town a Boulder, in February a 1922, an I started perty soon goin to the Copper School, I never saw Catherine Bosworth ennymore. But what's funny is that her Pa was Ed Bosworth, an Ed Bosworth was the game warden. Later I saw a *lot* a Ed Bosworth.

Imagine that! Ed Bosworth's daughter Catherine had been my girl-friend! An Ed Bosworth was the game warden an the man I feared above all men.

Some things are jest too doggone funny.

Movin to the Town a Boulder, on February 22, 1922, wasn't very funny, though. Pa had got himself a job in Kinzel's sawmill right away when we came from North Dakota. I kin understand that we couldn't stay forever with Grampa an Gramma in their brick house—we were jest too big a family for that—but why we had ta come out to a vacant house in the Town a Boulder, with no firewood, on February 22, is a mystery ta me.

I'd guess it was about a eight-mile trip. Pa hired a fella who had a team a horses an a bobsled, an after we'd loaded the sled, we headed out ta Boulder. There was Pa, the fella drivin the team, my sister Mary, an me. The rest of 'em stayed behind, for a week or so.

I was ten years old, jest barely. I didn't have enny proper winter clothes. All I had on my feet was a pair a socks an those ankle-high shoes I'd got when we left Dawson. It was so cold I couldn't stand ta ride the bobsled. So I walked every step a the way to that empty house in Boulder.

The sun was goin down when we arrived. First we had ta unload the cookstove, set it up, find some wood ta burn, an build a fire. When the bobsled was unloaded, the man who'd brought us out headed back ta town. By then it was dark.

Next morning, Pa found some boards, cobbled up a pair a skis, an began cuttin a few dead trees for firewood. The snow was up to my butt.

How we survived those first few days in that cold house is a mystery ta me. But we did. An I been livin in the Town a Boulder ever since. Maybe somethin in my brain got froze. There has got ta be a explanation somewhere.

It was a week, probably, before Ma an the rest a the kids came out from town. An, when they did come, they rode the loggin train from Jensen an got off at the 27 landing, which was about a mile north a where our rented house was located, an then they had ta walk.

We didn't have enny horse at the time. No horse, no cow, no chickens, no nothin.

Well, we all had cold feet, so I spoze you could say we each had somethin. I had got mine when Old Man Lucier had brought us out with his bobsled, an I ain't sure I still didn't have 'em when summer rolled around.

Within a day or so, Pa was helpin a man named Eric Nelson load cordwood on railroad cars, at the landing. Now Eric Nelson lived in

Jensen, or he had a house there, but he stayed in a shack right close to the 27 landing, an loadin cordwood was his job.

Cordwood was firewood in four-foot lengths, mostly hard maple. People burned a lot a wood those days, an they wanted the good stuff, not like now when they don't know the difference between popple an piss elm. An my Pa helped Eric Nelson load cars.

Perty soon all us kids—well, all that were old enuff, ennyway, Mary, Clara, Daisy'n me—were walkin the other direction ta go ta school. We had about a two-mile walk each way, all on unplowed roads—there was no snow plowin those years, none at all—an in the spring, when the snow melted, there was a long alder swamp the road went through, on the south side a the hill we called Sandy Boehner, an the water was over the road an we'd have ta take off our shoes'n socks an wade for most of a quarter mile through that ice cold water.

Now Old Man Boehner was a bachelor who lived near the hill on the north end a that swamp, an we called that hill "Sandy" becuz it *was* sand an, later, when I got old enuff ta have a car, I'd really have ta giv'er all she had ta git up that hill without gettin stuck in the sand.

That spring a 1922, when the snow melted and it rained a lot, the basement of the Copper School flooded, an there were toilets in the cellar—not the flushin kind either—so you kin imagine what that was like, what the smell was. I think that school had only been built the year before, I ain't sure, but they hired several men, an one of 'em was Old Man Karban, ta dig a trench an drain that cellar, an they jest put in drain tiles while they were at it.

I walked ta school in those same ankle-high shoes I'd come from Dawson in, the same ones I'd walked in followin that bobsled. I think my feet were *always* cold.

The brightest spot that spring was findin red berries in a swamp jest south a the rented house. We took 'em ta Ma an she looked at 'em an she sez, "Those are wintergreen berries. They're good ta eat." Did we ever pick the berries! We'd a eaten the whole plant, if we cudda.

Before the spring was out, Ma had a cow and a flock a chickens. Don't ask me where they came from, cuz I don't know. But, those days, havin a cow and a flock a chickens was a necessity, an there was a old log barn by that rented house, so there was a place ta put'em. Pa had ta buy hay, and grain, too.

I don't recall that Ma ever put in a garden by that rented place. See, Pa, before we'd come out in February, had already bought forty acres a land, with two arms a the Boulder River runnin through it, about a quarter-mile north a the 27 landing, an there was a flat maybe a eighth of a mile east a where our house got put (I know I'm gettin ahead a myself here, Seedy, but I can't help it, that's what happens when ya drive a old horse an the lines are slack), an in that flat my Ma put in a garden.

Now whether that garden got planted in the summer a '22, or in the summer a '23, I ain't sure. We lived through the winter a '22 an '23, so there had ta be food from somewhere.

Well, let me try'n tell ya somethin so all this ain't so confusin.

The train that came out ta Boulder was a loggin train, a steamer. It wasn't unusual for that train ta come through twice a day, goin up empty, comin back loaded. An by loaded, I mean up ta twenty cars full a sawed logs.

So those loggin camps up ta the northwest, by six, seven, ten miles, had ta a been *busy*.

An there was our local landing, an it's there Pa helped Eric Nelson load cordwood. Small-time jobbers would bring logs in ta get loaded onto railroad cars there, too. It was a busy place.

See, the big pine was gone, taken out already. Nothin but stumps when it came ta pine. White pine, I mean, big ones. Three, four feet on the stump some of'em.

Those logs had been floated down the Boulder. That was before my time, but not by much. An that flat where Ma made her garden had been a landing for rollin pine inta the river. It was real level an had only a little brush. So it was perty easy ta clear. An that garden was big, I kin tell you that, cuz I spent lots a time down there hoein, an all the kids that could tell the difference between a weed an a carrot did, too.

But I'm tryin ta draw ya the big pitcher here, so I gotta draw a little here an a little there an maybe perty soon you kin see if it's a horse I'm drawin or jest a horse's hind end.

Ennyway, in the summer a '22 the county put a road buildin crew on a stretch a road that started about a half-mile north a our rented place, about where the town hall now sits, an they worked north, acrost the railroad track, down to an acrost the river—both arms a the river, cuz there were two old narrow bridges in there already, an they jest left'em alone—an on the far side, in a flat at the base a Karban Hill, which is acrost the road from where Oscar Weaver'n me opened the gravel pit some years later, the county kept a road camp. In that flat. Tents fer the men.

Now why the county worked *north* a where the town hall now sits, rather than south, I do not know, cuz the road goin *south* a that spot was hardly more'n a dog trail, an by rights they should a done that first.

But I ain't here ta tell ya what *should a happened*, I'm here ta tell ya what *did*.

An there was a bunkhouse, built on skids, jest sittin off ta one side, near the landing. It was maybe forty feet long, an it wasn't bein used. The county crew was stayin in tents, in that far flat, acrost both bridges ta the north. They never used that bunkhouse. Some loggin outfit owned it, an there it sat.

Now the county crew was all men an horses, except for one big old Cat called a "Sixty." An that big Cat pulled a big old grader they used for ditchin. Pa had a job drivin a team a horses for the county, pullin a slusher.

Now maybe ya don't know what a slusher is, so I better tell ya.

A slusher, ta be real basic, is a wheelbarrow without a wheel. It's got a pair a wooden handles, like a wheelbarrow, but it gets pulled along by a team a horses. The front edge is a little sharp, an by liftin the handles, as the horses are pullin, the slusher bites inta the ground an fills with dirt. When it's full, ya push the handles down—it's all musclepower—an the whole contraption slides along on its belly until ya git ta where ya want ta dump it, an then ya got to lift both handles way up high an the dirt dumps out.

It ain't like pushin dirt with a bulldozer, or diggin with a backhoe. This was slow, hard work.

Pa wasn't a teamster. I kin remember watchin him in a long line a men an horses, all of 'em workin slushers, an his lines were always slack, an that ain't no way ta drive a team. But he kept at it.

I don't think I knew Pa'd bought that worthless forty until he also bought that empty bunkhouse. Us kids weren't told that kind a stuff. Parents then didn't tell their kids much, an they certainly didn't ask their opinions, as they sometimes do now. Ennyway, I was there watchin as that "Sixty" Cat pulled the bunkhouse down ta our land. It probably was the end a summer, 1922, when all that started ta come together.

Right away Pa added onto that bunkhouse, stuck a kitchen on the north end, an put up some room dividers. We were in there by the fall.

We never had a well. There were two springs, one on our land an one acrost the road, an Pa boxed both of'em, an that's where we got our water.

I'm gonna tell ya one more thing, an then I'm gonna shut up for a while. You kin only stir these memories up so much before the water starts gettin kind a cloudy. Then you gotta wait fer things ta settle. That's how I'm startin ta feel. Too many things stirred up. Getting murky.

Ennyway, when we moved inta that bunkhouse an outa that rented house, a family by the name a Kortholtz moved in behind us. That man an my Pa sawed logs together the next winter, an Mrs. Kortholtz was gonna have a baby. When the time came, Ma went over ta be Mrs. Kortholtz's midwife. An when she came back, Ma said Mrs. Kortholtz had told'er that this new baby was her twenty-third.

Now we were a big family an gettin bigger—there'd be thirteen kids by the time Pa an Ma were done makin babies—but *twenty-three* kids!

If we were poor an barely gettin by, what in the world were those folks livin on? It astonished me jest ta think about it. Did then, still does.

That first summer, the summer a '22, I had ta bum around the neighborhood, a course, an meet such neighbors as there were. Part at that was watchin the county road crew at work, an goin ta visit their road camp.

That camp was in a little clearing at the foot a Karban Hill, right next ta the Boulder River. Our property line went right through that clearing somewheres, so some a that camp must a been on Old Man Karban's land an some of it on Pa's. Whether either of'em got enny rent from the county I do not know.

It was a busy little place. There was a bunkhouse for the men, and a cook shanty, a horse barn—all that kind a stuff, though none of it was made out a lumber. Just brown tents. Like I think I said, the county had one big Cat they used for ditchin, otherwise everything was done with horses an with men.

A course on the Fourth a July they shut'er down. But somebody had ta take care a the horses, feed an water'em. Old Man Karban's oldest son Mike got that job. I'm guessin he was eighteen, nineteen years old, kind of a reckless cuss who had a little bit of a stutter. I liked his swagger, ya know. I was just ten years old. So I hung around with'em whenever I could, followed'em around like a puppy.

Mike sometimes carried a pistol, an a course that fascinated me. But on the Fourth, Mike showed up with a single-barrelled shotgun. After he'd taken care a the horses, he went over ta where the county crew kept their dynamite, picked out a stick, an set it up against a big old pine stump. Then he backed up thirty, forty yards an shot that stick a dynamite with his shotgun. I was behind'em, watchin.

When Mike pulled the trigger that dynamite blew, an a big hunk a stump practically disappeared. He only did it once.

As far as I know, he never got in enny trouble for that prank. The county men noticed right away that the stump had been blown, an it didn't take'em long ta figger out that Mike Karban was the one who'd done it. I guess they jest took it as a joke. Or maybe they figgered blowin stumps with a shotgun an a stick a dynamite was a patriotic thing ta do on the Fourth a July.

Ma knit all winter. Socks an mittens. She also sewed our shirts. But when spring rolled around, she was in her garden, down in the flat.

I'm gonna say that garden was maybe three acres, but she planted her rows wide enuff so that Old Jack, our skinny, tired horse, could pull a one-horse cultivator between the rows. I held the handles and followed that cultivator up an down those rows for miles, seemed like. When I wasn't cultivatin I was hoein. I think I had blisters clear up ta my elbows.

In the summer that's all Ma did was garden an can. An she didn't just send us kids down ta the garden, either. She was there. She worked an we worked.

I think if it hadn't been fer her garden, her cannin, we'd a all starved ta death. Pa'd put a partial cellar under the bunkhouse, and those cellar shelves were full a her jars. There was no refrigeration, other than what cold weather provided. No gas stoves. No 'lectric lights. No runnin water. We were poor. Everything was real basic.

When there were raspberries, we picked raspberries. Same with blueberries an wild strawberries. Once a bunch a us kids was out pickin wild strawberries, maybe a mile from home, in what was spozed ta be a field but was actually a rough pasture jest loaded with big old pine stumps, an all of a sudden I felt kinda funny an looked up an there, maybe fifty feet away, was a timber wolf jest standin there lookin at me with those strange far-seein eyes that seem like they're lookin right through you and, at the same time, pullin ya in—like one a those—what a ya call'em?—hypnotists.

I'd been down on my hands an knees, but I stood up real fast, kind a shaky, an that wolf jest turned an walked away, like we maybe weren't worth the trouble eatin, too skinny an full a bones, an I jest stood there with my mouth hangin open.

It might a been that year Ma canned thirty-two quarts a wild strawberries. I believe that was her record.

Ma wasn't enny housekeeper, but she could go out an saw wood with a crosscut saw, jest like a man. She had'er own little 410 shotgun, an lots a times, early in the mornin or toward evenin, when those birds were out at the edge a the road pickin gravel, she'd go an shoot partridges. Never flyin. She always swatted'em on the ground. But she got'em. An we ate'em.

Once I was out lookin for the cows—they never were fenced—an I came over this little hill an there on the other side was one a those timber wolves standin there lookin at me. I turned an run home, or maybe I flew, an Ma came back with me, carrying her 410, but that wolf was gone. If she'd a seen'em, she'd a shot'em, though probably that little 410'd only have tickled his hide an made'em laugh.

We hadn't been in the bunkhouse but a year or so an Pa was sick of it an wanted ta go back ta Dakota. Ma wasn't enny sort a bossy woman, but she said no, we ain't goin, an she meant it. An we didn't go.

So when Pa worked out, which he did when he could, when there was work, a little somethin here an a little somethin there, I was the biggest boy an had ta cut wood for the stoves. Cookstove in the kitchen. Heater stove in the middle of the house. There were rampikes, old dead trees standin up like scarecrows all over the place, an I had a dull old saw, an there were lots a days I stayed home from school ta cut firewood.

We had a shack of a barn, three cows, maybe, a flock a chickens, an usually some geese. Ma tried turkeys again, but for some reason that never worked. They wouldn't live. Pa'd usually buy two little pigs in the spring, an we'd feed'em out till late in the fall, butcher'em, and have pork for the winter. Or until it ran out.

I remember we had a female collie called Gyp, an there were always a few cats in the barn. Gyp was more or less my dog, an when I'd pick up Pa's old single-shot .22 ta go shoot at rabbits, she'd get excited an was ready ta go.

There were lots a snowshoe rabbits those days, lots of'em, an there were several swamps ta hunt'em in. One a those swamps was a cedar swamp on the east end a Eric Nelson's eighty, but the branches of the cedars grew right down ta the ground, so it was hard ta see, hard ta get a shot. So I went more offen to a alder swamp on the other side a the railroad track, an I'd jest find me a place ta stand among the alders an old Gyp'd start sniffin around an perty soon—"Yip, yip, yip"—she'd a smelled one or seen one an I'd jest wait. She wasn't a good rabbit hound. She'd get kind a crazy an go runnin every which a way, but that was okay, cuz sooner or later one a those rabbits would hop inta view, in no big hurry, an I'd get a shot.

We ate lots a rabbits. Got ta the point where I despised the sight a one. What I didn't shoot I snared. An once, before I could go ta school in the dead a winter, Ma made me go down ta the cedar swamp an let Gyp out of a snare I'd set for rabbits. We could hear her barkin down there, in that cold, frosty air, an whinin. So I had ta go get her loose.

I think the hardest test fer Gyp came when I'd been walkin down the railroad track, in the spring, with a boy named George Eberhardt. George was a year younger'n me, an he lived with his family down by the Wisconsin River, maybe a mile an a half or two miles away. (It was George's Pa who had the old skow that Old Pete Peterson had used ta lay down on, drunk, an paddle himself home acrost the Wisconsin River.) Ennyway, we were walkin down the track an there, stuck between the rails, was a baby woodchuck. It had got in somehow, but it wasn't big enough ta get out. Couldn't climb over the rails. So I caught it.

Well, at first it tried awful hard ta get away. But I jest held it, gentle like, an perty soon that little woodchuck snuggled up in my arms an fell asleep. An, while it was sleepin, I carried it home.

A course when I got back all the kids wanted ta hold'em, an so he got passed around from hand ta hand an arm ta arm. An when we brought'em inta the house, Pa sez "Turn'em loose."

So we took'em outside an turned'em loose. But that little stinker followed us right back inta the house. Pa bent down an picked'em up, an we thought "Oh, oh, now there's trouble," but perty soon Pa liked'em, too. In fact, it got ta where, when we'd sit ta eat, that woodchuck'd come sit on its haunches by Pa's chair an let out a shrill whistle. Pa'd reach down with a crust a bread, an that woodchuck'd scramble away somewheres ta have his lunch, too.

Now Gyp was death on woodchucks, but we told'er "No" in a way she knew we meant it. An we sat with'em both fer a while an worked it out, an perty soon that woodchuck an that dog were best a friends. They'd lay there chewin on each other, the little woodchuck bitin Gyp on the lips, an Gyp putting her whole mouth over the little woodchuck's head, an perty soon the woodchuck'd scoot off to a hole she had, or he had, right by the barn, an then it'd be nap time.

But then, after a while, George Eberhardt kept comin around and he kinda ragged at us that that woodchuck was his, too, count a we'd been together when it was caught, even if I was the one who'd caught it. George wanted his share, ya might say, his turn, an finally Pa got tired a the naggin an sez ta me, "Give it ta George."

So I did. Didn't like to, didn't want to, but I did. I gave that little woodchuck ta George.

So George took it home, an I never saw the woodchuck again. I think his dog killed it.

Ya know, I honestly can't recall if there were frogs in Dawson. There must a been, with all those sloughs, but I jest can't bring it ta mind. That was almost a hunnerd years ago, ya know, an maybe frogs weren't invented then, yet. Or maybe those frogs have buried themselves so deep in the mud a my memories they can't remember how ta crawl out. Hard ta say. I'm jest this bent, old stalk a seein, an there's some things that escape my attention.

But there was a feelin that came over a person, come spring, I mean, here in Boulder. It might a been mud—at least the road was mud, an some a the area right around the house an barn was mud—but that everlastin snow was finally gone, an on those heavy, misty, cloudy days even the woodsmoke out a the chimney kind a laid down over the roof an rubbed up against the budding bushes and brown grass, wantin ta be green.

The bunkhouse was close ta the river, an when the ice went out you woke to the roarin of the water an that's how ya went ta sleep. Seems like everything was movin, wantin ta get somewhere, wakin up, itchin for a little fun. There were geese headed north, ragtag bands a ducks—an a few of 'em would land in the river an splash an duck their heads in the water—an redwing blackbirds trillin from the cattails, an perty soon the killdeer.

An ta all a this there was a constant choir a frogs, all kinds a frogs, all of 'em tryin ta sing louder'n everybody else, until yer eardrums got ta hummin an buzzin an ya hardly knew ennymore whether those frogs were outside a yer head or in.

Have ya ever been drunk on spring? I think I was.

Now remember, there wasn't enny television, no radio, no cars goin up an down the road, no airplanes in the sky, no 'lectric lights. None a that. What we had was a patched-up old bunkhouse, a woodburnin cookstove, a flock a kids, a shack of a barn an some critters glad ta have come through the winter alive, an right outside the door we had *Nature*.

Now there was a railroad track about a quarter-mile to the south, an there were rollways a logs at the landing, an there were stumps an acres a brush, but even that dreariness was kind a magical when all those birds were singin an actin up, an the swamploads a frogs were givin'er all they had. You might still a had cold feet, wet an muddy ta boot, but there was *life* out there everywhere an it plain made ya dizzy ta be out in it.

I think it was the river that was the boss. I mean, there was all this stuff goin on—frogs singin, ducks scootin after one another in the little backwaters, redwing blackbirds trillin out their territory—but the river didn't have enny time for nothin but a big mighty rush. It was in a hurry, maybe jest for the hell of it, jest for the fun of it, but it was *goin*.

That river fascinated me. That river was *alive*.

I think it was Clara who discovered there were fish in the river. We had us a fish spear—don't ask me where it came from, cuz I don't know—an Clara took it out one day an when she came back she was carryin a couple a speared northerns with'er.

An that sort a opened things up.

But ya had ta get used ta bein in the river, an when we came ta live there, by the Boulder, none of us kids could swim. An that was a problem, a real impediment. How are ya gonna be *in* the river if yer *afraid* of it?

Now Clara was the bold one, the daring one, an she'd offen drag Daisy along with 'er on some escapade, or maybe Daisy jest refused ta be left behind. I don't know.

But it was in the summer, an the river was high from rain, an Clara an Daisy an me were down at the second bridge, the far bridge, lookin at the water. An Clara jest started jumpin off the bridge into the river, an the current would wash'er on down real quick, an after she'd been swept along fifty, sixty, a hunnerd feet, she'd catch hold of a brush hangin out over the water an she'd pull herself back ta shore.

She did that two, three, four times, ya know, with that ain't-I-somethin, yer-a-chickenshit, devil-may-care look in'er eyes, an perty soon it's Clara *an* Daisy doin it, jumpin off the bridge, an, ya know, a boy kin only stand so much a that bein left out, bein put ta shame like that, even if ya are half scared ta death, an it wasn't too much longer an it's *all three of us* jumpin off that bridge an gettin swept downstream an pullin ourselves inta shore by grabbin onta the brush.

I spoze we cudda drowned, all three of us. But we didn't. An I'll tell ya somethin else. We learned ta swim that day. Maybe not real good, exactly, but we learned the basics. We got rid a our fear.

See, the current took ya off a yer feet. Jest swept ya down. There was no standin there in water up ta yer belly, tryin ta get the courage to lay down flat an try a little tame dog paddlin. None a that. The current jest swept us along an maybe it was sheer fear or desperation that got ya ta move yer hands an arms an legs in the right way, but we came out a that situation *swimmin*.

After that, we were *ready* for the river, an there was nothin ta hold us back.

There ain't a lot ta tell ya about the years between the fall a '22, when we moved inta the bunkhouse down by the Boulder, an the spring a 1926, when I graduated from grade school, high school, an college, all on the same day.

Ya see, I was extra smart, so they rushed me right through.

I mean, there's probably a lot ta tell, but there was a routine, an I was a kid, an I jest fit inta that routine. That sort a thing begins ta fade from view.

Pa worked where he could, sometimes in loggin camps. Ma did her gardenin an cannin an sewin and knittin an endless cookin an addin another baby every couple a years, an us kids had our jobs an we did'em. There was sickness, but never too serious, so nobody died. We were a healthy, tough lot. Sometimes there was hardly enuff ta eat—nobody was fat, I'll tell ya that—but we made it. I don't know how we did, but we did it.

Lookin back now, when there's a furnace in the basement an the winter's wood is dry an all stacked, an there's 'lectric lights an runnin water an a freezer an a refrigerator an all the food we want ta eat, an a car in the garage, an the roads are plowed, an Uncle Sam sends me a check every month, I really do wonder how in the world we lived through those years. An that was *before* the Depression!

Man, oh, man! Some things are beyond explanation.

But I know yer lookin fer some little stories, Seedy, kind a like a little heap a scratchins a cat does over his business, so I'll see what I kin drag up. "Little head, little wit"—but you heard that one before.

I think I told ya the train brought Ma out from town, her'n all the rest a the kids, when Pa an Mary an me'd been in that rented house about a week. End a February, beginnin a March, 1922. Somethin like that.

Now that train was a loggin train, wasn't enny sort a passenger train, an there were loggin camps further up in the woods, way on up the rail line. An those lumberjacks—some of 'em, ennyway—jest *had* ta get ta town on a Saturday night ta drink up their wages or visit a certain cat in a cathouse, though some of 'em, I'm sure, were family men an jest went home. Had ta be one or two like that, ennyway.

Now those loggin camps worked six days a week, Monday through Saturday. An Saturday evenin, about six o'clock, the train'd head up ta the camps, goin past our place, with one or two coaches hooked on behind. So those men'd eat supper at the camps, get on the train, an head inta Jensen ta do whatever it was they were gonna do. Git their heads swelled up with booze. Find a kitty ta pet.

If Pa was workin in one a them camps, he'd get let off at the landing an walk on home.

Monday mornin, about six o'clock, Pa'd be back at the landing with a little kerosene lantern, which he'd slowly start swinging back'n forth as the train came inta view, headed up. The train'd stop, Pa'd hand the lantern ta Ma or one of us kids, an he'd get on the train for another week in the woods.

During the week there was no passenger coach, though there was usually a caboose tied behind the log cars. So I suspect that if somebody got real sick or hurt bad they'd take'em out in the caboose. But that wudda been an emergency, not a regular sort a thing.

We never rode the train for gettin ta town. If ya needed ta get ta town fer groceries, ya hooked Old Jack to a little cutter an drove'em— though ya didn't drive'em hard, cuz he was a slow old plug, not fed enuff, an so it took two an a half, maybe three hours jest ta get ta town. I did that many, many times.

I'd take Jack to the livery stable in the Sixth Ward, which is what everybody called that piece a Jensen on the west side a the Wisconsin River, give Jack a armful a poor hay I'd brought along, an go ta Staats' store with a list that Ma'd given me. If I had enny money, I'd buy me a lunch there, an eat it right in the store. Once I ate some dried fish, an when old Staats charged me thirty-five cents I was shocked. I had the money, an I paid'em, but then I was broke. Once again.

See, Staats put the groceries on a bill, an that bill'd get paid by an by. When the folks went ta Washington in '36, Ma wrote ta me an said ta sell the forty acres she an Pa owned. So I did. Sold it ta Mark Lemmer for three hunnerd dollars. But Ma'd also said ta pay the bill at Staats' store. So I did that, too. Wasn't much left a that three hunnerd dollars ta send ta Ma. Three hunnerd dollars was a lot a money in the Depression. So old Staats had carried the folks a long time.

It took most of a mornin ta get ta town, almost all afternoon ta get home. Ya didn't run ta town on a whim those days, or ta get a ice cream cone, or ta go see a movie, or ta go *bowling*. Eighty years ago an it might as well a been eight hunnerd, as little now as ennybody kin understand what it was like. Amazing.

Ennyway, us kids did mostly get hauled ta school. We were over three miles from school, an Harry Eberhardt had the job a haulin us sometimes. In the winter he'd drive a horse an a sled with some sort a homemade cab stuck on it, an when the weather was warmer, when the roads were passable, he'd take us in a old Model T. Sometimes there were the Karban kids ta haul, too, but the Karbans were an unstable family so sometimes there'd be kids ta haul an sometimes not.

One year—an this was probably when I was in the eighth grade, gettin ready ta graduate from college, ya know—an there was bickerin in the town about havin ta haul those Buckberry kids. It was jest a local school board, ya know—years later I even got ta be clerk, which is a interestin way a gettin yerself a headache—an so people could raise a little hell if they wanted to, an probably there was people who didn't like the extra expense a haulin us ta school. Too many, too far, too poor, whatever it was. Too dumb.

So that year we had ta walk. There were always more an more of us, an in the winter—no decent winter clothes or boots or nothin—it was jest too far, too cold, too much snow for the littler kids ta walk. An so it got ta be my job ta get up early in the mornin, feed'n harness Old Jack, hook'em to a open sled, an drive the kids ta school. About three miles.

Now the Copper School was right on the corner where Mail Route Road butted inta the county road, an up Mail Route about a quarter-mile a man named Clarence Sayers had a little ragged farm an he had a shed jest wide enough fer me ta put Old Jack in. So I'd drop the kids off at school, go on down ta Sayers' place, unhook the sled, unharness Old Jack, give'em a bit a hay I'd brought along, squeeze'em inta that narrow shed, an hurry back ta school.

Emma Nelson was the teacher. She was the daughter a Eric Nelson, who'd hired Pa ta load cordwood on the railroad cars when we first came out ta Boulder. Emma Nelson boarded jest down the road at Lansbachs' place, so she didn't have far ta come ta school. An she knew we were poor. Maybe that's why she'd always tell me ta go throw wood down the cellar an then stack it. I did that time an again, always in the afternoon when the other kids were studyin. Or spozed ta be studyin. An every time she'd give me a quarter.

By the eighth grade, I'd perty much learned what there was ta be learned at the Copper School. Readin an writin an arithmetic were no problem. But I never could get that "language" stuff—"adverbs" an "pronouns" an all that crap. When it came ta that, I was lost, an I never did find me a compass.

There were maybe twenty kids in the entire school, all eight grades, but it was always me Emma Nelson asked ta throw an stack the wood. An I always did it, an she always gave me a quarter.

The only other money I made was from trappin weasels. They get pure white, ya know, in the winter, except for that little black tip on the end a their tails. An since I'd learned ta trap gophers in Dakota, I thought I'd give it a try on weasels.

Mostly I'd set traps in culverts, on the way ta school. An one a the first weasels I caught was also one a the biggest I ever caught. It was somethin like thirty inches long, from the nose to the tip a the tail. I ain't never seen one bigger. On one a those trips ta town for groceries with Old Jack (I had him tucked away eatin poor hay in the livery stable), I walked acrost the bridges over the Wisconsin River an went ta see Abey Block, an Abey said it was the biggest weasel *he'd* ever seen.

Abey gave me three dollars for that skin. Three dollars! Why most guys were only earnin twenty cents a hour! I felt like a rich man, I tell you, even if I only was a kid.

But there were lots a weasels around becuz there were lots a rabbits. See, if there's lots a rabbits around, there'll be weasels. If there's no rabbits, then there's no weasels, ya know.

I don't know if the rabbit eats the weasel or the weasel eats the rabbit. I jest don't know. An I never figured out how ta—what do ya call it?—*diagram* that sentence.

Maybe I gotta get out my paint brush, so ta speak, an draw some more pitchers on the barn wall. So whoever is followin this story kin figger out which way is up. Whichever way that is. If yer a Chinaman, "up" is the opposite a here. Or so they say. I ain't ever been in China ta see for myself.

Ennyway, the Town a Boulder is a double town, meanin it's twice as big as a town needs ta be ta be, well, legal, I spoze.[1] An most of the people were—still are—on the south end. Nobody is spozed ta live year-round in the northern part now, jest deer an bear, skunks an timber wolves up in the county forest, but when I was a kid there were loggin camps up there an, later, there was a sprinklin a people in shacks an whatnot. Even Cigarbox Smitty an his homemade fiddle. But that comes later. I ain't told ya about him yet.

---

1. A "town" in Wisconsin is supposed to be, at minimum, thirty-six square miles. The Town of Boulder is seventy-two. S. B.

Mail Route road headed north off the county road an went about two miles north a the Copper School, before it butted inta the railroad track an quit. Harry Eberhardt lived up there, between the track an the Wisconsin River.

The county road went north a where we lived in that bunkhouse by the Boulder River, went north about a mile, up past Karban Hill, an then it went west an north in a bunch a steps, crossin the Boulder River twice more, an Pa got ta work on the buildin a both a those bridges. It was the sort a work he liked. But when it was done, it was done, an he had ta go back ta lookin under rocks fer work.

He sawed logs now an then, but he wasn't no lumberjack. He jest never fit in.

An then the county road, when it had gone west an north a bunch a steps, turned due east an lit out for the Wisconsin River. That due east part was about six miles long, an in the middle, sort of, a road now comes up from the south, a road (my paintbrush is runnin out a paint, Seedy)—a road that kin be driven year-round now but, when I was a kid, wasn't even there.

Well, the south end was there. If ya want ta call it a road. That road started where the county road turned west, about a mile north a our bunkhouse. An there were a couple a bachelors lived up that road who made their livin, such as it was, from huntin and trappin. Their names were Reinhold Kleinschmidt and Harry Krause. An beyond them was an abandoned homestead everybody called the Anderson Place.

Now when I say "road," Seedy, ya gotta use yer imagination, cuz that "road," like lots a other so-called "roads," had two crooked ruts an a face-slappin whiplash a overhangin brush. There weren't no stop signs or speed limits or pedestrian crosswalks, I kin tell ya that—only tracks where a deer might a walked acrost the road, or a bear, maybe. Mud when it rained, dust when it didn't, an snow up ta yer butt in the winter. No plowing.

Whoever had punched in that trail, back before my time, must a done it in the winter, an they must a had a sense a humor, becuz they gave it a name that stuck. They called it Frostbite Avenue.

Now years later, early thirties maybe, a road got punched inta the west a the county road, down by the folks' bunkhouse, an that was a dead-ender put in in the heat a summer, an the name they gave that road was Heatstroke Lane.

That name stuck, too, but jest barely. Lots a folks thought "Heatstroke Lane" was kind a copycattin "Frostbite Avenue," tryin ta be cute, ya know, an cute doesn't have a lot a traction when yer jest tryin ta eke out a livin in the brush.

Ennyway, I'm tellin you all this, paintin this pitcher, cuz I was gettin ta be a big boy—voice changin, hair growin in places it hadn't been growin before, a real college graduate—an I started pokin around more an more, gettin ta know people, stickin my nose out.

Funny how that works. The world is all fresh an ripe for explorin as a fella starts ta feel his oats. Later, when those oats are planted, he works his ass off jest ta keep it all together. An, later yet, some old codger goes ta sleep in his chair an looks out the window with hardly a twinge a ambition. Maybe his oats got moldy.

Life is a funny thing. Those who think they know all about it don't know nothin. Life's a mystery. Life's a miracle. If there's one thing I know for sure it's that I *don't* know. An that's fer certain.

3

Deadhead Poverty PhD

Ya don't hear much about kids runnin away from home ennymore. Maybe most kids don't. Maybe most kids never did. But I was one that did.

I did it in the fall a 1926, same year as I graduated with a graduate degree in Poverty Management. Doctor Poor, they called me. Paid real good.

It's hard ta find a job like that ennymore. Kind a obsolete. But jest wait a while an poor'll come back in style. It might be a little hard ta get used to, but it has a way a fittin in. Only takes a little while ta adjust.

If I'm still around when the goin gets rough, I kin help ya do that adjustin. I had lots a experience. The fees are reasonable. Jest remember: Doctor Poor, Reasonable an Thorough. You'll find me in the phone book, in the Yella Pages, under "Adjustments." I think I'll teach people how ta get poor an avoid the rush. In fact, come to think of it, that'll be my motto—Get Poor Now, Avoid the Rush. How about it, Seedy? Want to invest in Poverty Management? Bound ta be awful good returns.

Ennyway, graduatin from the Copper School wasn't like graduatin now. Now the kids get gowns an goofy hats an diplomas an gifts an a party an everybody treats'em like they're really somebody or really accomplished somethin. Big joke.

I had ta walk ta town an take an examination at the old high school, an when I was done I had ta walk home. Figger twenty miles round trip. That's what I did fer "graduation." I was fourteen years old.

Sometime in that year, I guess, a family by the name a Batchelder moved inta the neighborhood—past us, past Karban Hill, up around the corner by about three-quarters of a mile, on the south side a the county road, on the east side a the river, next ta one of the bridges my Pa'd help build.

The old man's name was Al, an first he owned two forties, an then he bought a third. Him an the bank, probably.

An eventually I bought one a those forties. But we ain't up ta that part yet.

The reason Al Batchelder bought the third forty was that he put up a log house an, without knowin it, built it right over the line on a forty he didn't own. When he figgered it out, he had ta go buy that other forty, which happened ta be for sale, jest so he could have his house on his own land.

So he had two forties south a the county road, which is where his log house was, an one forty to the north.

It's the north one I bought later.

Ennyway, there was a bunch a kids in that family, an three of 'em especially figgered inta my life. First there was a older boy named Howard. He had a wreck of a car, an he took me along fishin. We went up to a lake near Tomahawk—we didn't catch ennything—but we got there by takin the county road up that set a steps north and west an then due east to the Wisconsin River. I'd never been on that due-east piece a road before—it was brand new—an it was jest a dog trail carved out like a tunnel, with big overhangin trees, mostly hemlock, on either side a the road.

When we were done catchin nothin at the lake, we ended up goin through Jensen on our way home. Howard didn't have enny muffler on his old junker, an I thought we'd get stopped fer sure. But we didn't.

I'm gonna mention Gladys next, but I ain't gonna explain about her now. She ain't in no hurry ennymore, ennyway. She kin jest wait a while.

So now I'm gettin up to the runnin away part. There was another Batchelder kid who figgers in, an that was Victor, who was near my own age. An it was him an me that ran away together. Neither of us told our folks ennything. We jest got on our bicycles an went.

I don't know where Victor got his bicycle, but I got mine from a guy named Engelbeck who ran a dry goods store in the Sixth Ward. I'd learned ta ride on George Eberhardt's bicycle. So I already was a kind a perfessional. I think I paid Engelbeck twelve dollars for that bike.

Don't ask me where I got the money. I was a tight old bugger even as a kid. If I had a chance ta make a nickle or a dime, I always did it. So I guess I saved an saved until I had enuff ta buy that bicycle.

We didn't know what ta do with ourselves, Victor an me. Out a school. No job. No longer kids. But not yet grown men. We both came from big families, an there wasn't much peace in that. We were anxious ta *do* somethin, an one of us spotted an ad in the paper. Somebody wanted help on a farm, down past Wisconsin Rapids. So we decided ta go. An rather than tell our folks what we had in mind—figgerin, probably, they'd say it was stupid an tell us we couldn't—we jest left. Didn't tell nobody.

We made it ta Jensen, gettin dark already. That was the middle a September, somethin like that. We went ta the fairgrounds an slept on some hay in a cattle barn.

Next day we made it down past Wausau an stopped at a little farm an asked the farmer if we could sleep in his hay loft. Well, he looked us up an down an didn't say nothin, an then he finally asks, "You boys smoke?"

We said no an he said, "Okay, you kin sleep up in the mow." An so we did.

But he woke us early in the mornin an said it was time ta go. An so we went. Made it through Wisconsin Rapids an Nekoosa an Port Edwards an somewhere along in there was a homemade sign an a arrow an it said Help Wanted, Raking Cranberries, at a place called Cranmore.

So off we went, an we got ta this kind a rundown house late in the day, an there's a woman, maybe in her fifties, who's runnin the place. Jest her an another woman who was the cook.

Well, we tell her we're lookin for work, an she looks us over an asks us a bunch a questions, an it ain't long she knows more about us than we know about ourselves. An then she hired us. We ate in the house, three meals a day, but we slept on bunks in a little shack.

A man came out ta help next day. I guess he maybe was the foreman or somethin, an it was from him we learned ta rake cranberries. Everything was by hand. The cranberry beds were ragged an weedy, poorly taken care of, so it was real hard work. But we kept at it till the job was done—three, four weeks. Raked lots a berries.

When it was time ta flood the beds, the boss woman bought us boots an deducted that from our pay.

But she had a big Studebaker touring car, an once she said ta Victor an me, "I'm gonna take you boys for a ride." So she an the cook sat up front, put me an Victor in the back, an off she goes. It was a big car, a luxury car, an perty soon she calls back over her shoulder, "I'm gonna be doin eighty."

I don't know if she really went that fast, but the big Studebaker was goin down that dirt road like a bat out a hell. It was kind a fun, even if I was scared ta death.

After we were workin a while, a couple a Indian families came an put up their tipis. That about bugged out my eyes. I think they were from Black River Falls. The older man had a wife an a couple a little kids. The younger man jest had a wife. It was the older man we really got ta know. His name was Mike Red Cloud, an he was the friendliest man I ever met. In the evenin, he'd come over to the bunkhouse an jest sit an visit for a half-hour or so. Didn't swear. Didn't smoke. Didn't drink. Jest sit an visit with us boys. He really got ta be our friend.

It didn't take long ta realize Mike Red Cloud was also trappin muskrats. There were lots a pushups around, so I decided ta give it a try.[1] I'd trapped gophers in Dakota already, weasels up in Boulder, an I somehow got me a couple a traps, got up early in the mornin, went out an made some sets. I worked hard at it, but I never got a single rat.

Mike Red Cloud got'em though. I asked'em what he did with the carcass, after he'd skinned'em. "We eat'em," he said. An I guess they did. They didn't waste ennything.

While we were down there, I broke a pedal on my bike. So when the cranberries were done, we asked the younger Indian man—he had a car—if he'd drive us home. He said he would, an I think we paid'em six dollars. Maybe I cudda got my pedal fixed, I don't know. I think we weren't too enthused about bicyclin all that way back home. It was gettin colder, too.

Now there were never enny letters exchanged with the folks when we were down in the marsh. But I think the boss lady had got in touch

---

1. A "pushup" is what trappers call a mounded muskrat home in a marsh. They're made largely of mud and cattails. S. B.

with'em. I think our folks knew where we were. But we were, ya know, a little nervous about jest showin up at home. It was somethin we had ta face, but we weren't eager ta do it.

It was a easy ride back north. But when we were gettin perty close ta home, crossin the Copper River bridge an comin inta the Town a Boulder, I saw right away there was a house party goin on at John Allery's place, which was right close to the Copper River. We were still four, five miles from the folks' place.

"This is far enuff," I sez ta the Indian man who was drivin, an he let me an Victor out right there, bicycles an boots an whatever else we had. Wasn't much.

Well, it wasn't John Allery's place ennymore. John was a small man, a trapper, an his kids had come ta Copper School dressed in good winter clothes, wool an leather, real fine. I think the rest of us were a little envious, ya know. We didn't have ennything like that ta wear. John was a good trapper, an that's how he made his livin. Price for furs was high those days.

But John had a weakness for younger women. Some said cradle robbin. An I guess he pulled that trick one too many times, an his wife up an left him. Divorced him. An I guess that's why the place wasn't John Allery's ennymore.

Now it belonged ta Jake Snow, who was half Indian, an I liked Jake Snow. He was a middle-aged man, but he was my friend. Later—'29 maybe, somethin like that—Harry Eberhardt got a brand new car an George'd drive it everywhere, burn up the gas, ya know, so George an me went ta see Jake up on the reservation, outside a Woodruff. Jake was in tough shape by then, but he was glad ta see us, an his wife fixed us soup ta eat, which wasn't much, but I guess they didn't have much.

Now those little house parties—this was Prohibition, remember, an there wasn't spozed ta be enny liquor—those little parties always had moonshine at'em, somehow. An it didn't take long for me an Victor an a young man named Carl Marnholtz ta each chip in a quarter ta get us a small bottle a booze.

All I know is that I got drunker'n a fart an we ended up at Batchelders' for the night. But not before I got real belligerent with another part-Indian kid named John Edwards an even tried ta pick a fight with'em. Victor an Carl kind a pulled me away. Lookin back, I can't think a what cudda been in my mind ta do that ta John, unless I was takin out my worry on'em—worryin, I mean, about what the folks were gonna think a me when I got home, maybe what Pa'd try ta *do*.

A course the next day, big headed an feelin kind a champion stupid, I did have ta go home. It felt kind a funny. There weren't enny hard words spoken, but neither Ma nor Pa threw their arms around me, either. Ma never said ennything sweet about her Little Hobo. It's almost like they acted as if I hadn't been gone, at all. I don't think enny of us knew quite what ta say or do. Kind a awkward.

I guess I was too big ta get a lickin an too young ta treat like a man. Kind a stuck somewhere in-between.

I never did get that bicycle fixed. The pedal stayed broke. That bike might be layin down there in the weeds yet, for all I know.

Since I mentioned this kid by the name a John Edwards, the kid I picked a fight with—me an the moonshine an whatever else was worryin me about goin home—I spoze I should tell a little about his family, which is mostly about his Pa, though I did go ta school with John an his sister Dora, an there was a older sister whose name I can't remember who married one a Old Man Karban's older boys. An Dora later married Adolph Goetz, an Adolph delivered mail in the Town a Boulder.

Ennyway, John's Pa was Roy, an Roy was married to a woman who was part Indian. Some people called Roy a "Squawman," but I don't think ennybody said that to his face.

The family lived down near the Wisconsin River, in a house that was maybe a little better than a shack, not too far from John Allery's place. See, the Copper there is close ta runnin inta the Wisconsin, so the rivers are not far apart.

The Edwards family was already there when we moved inta the Town a Boulder. I ain't sure what Roy did for a livin, though he had a shack way up in the woods, next ta the Boulder River, but acrost the county road from what they now call Conservation Trail. An he had a little shed there for a team a horses. So maybe he did some roadwork or maybe he did a little loggin. I really don't know.

What Roy Edwards really did was *hunt*. He had one a those nifty contraptions that ya sit on an pump, an it starts ta scoot ya along on the railroad tracks. It was really made for two people ta operate, but one could do it by himself, an Roy did. An if you saw Roy, chances are you saw him an his rifle. He'd have it layin next to'em as he would be pumpin that little open car, goin kinda slow, always lookin, usually early in the mornin or late toward evenin, cuz that's when the deer are out, when they're movin. An then, maybe, you'd hear a shot. Usually jest one.

Harry Eberhardt told me that when he first moved into the Town a Boulder an got acquainted with Roy Edwards, Roy hired him ta pack out deer. Harry said Roy told'em, "No need fer you ta carry a gun," an all Harry did was haul deer. Twenty does, Harry said, jest in one fall. What Roy did with the bucks Harry never knew, though he figgered Roy was sellin'em somewhere.

Now the office men at Kinzel's lumbermill usta go huntin in the fall, an usually they'd take the train up to a loggin camp. Huntin fer them was like a fad, somethin ya had ta do, somethin ta brag about, a feather in yer cap. An usually they'd go home after a day or two, an they almost always had a nice buck ta take back an show off.

But those guys weren't hunters. So where'd they get the bucks?

Well, the story was that John Allery got a few, but John was more a trapper than a hunter. So they turned ta Roy Edwards, an Roy could shoot the bucks.

I kin only remember meetin Roy Edwards face ta face twice. First time I was only a kid. I'd been visitin George Eberhardt an I was comin home on the railroad track an there, all of a sudden, was Roy. An he had a rifle. I felt like I had ta say somethin, so I sez, "What kind a gun you got?"

Roy jest looked at me. An when he talked he talked way down low, ya had ta really listen ta hear what he was sayin, an he sez, "It's a Thirty Goverment, an it's good fer a mile, yet."

Second time I ran inta him was some years later. I was then a young man, startin ta hunt on my own, learnin how, an I was way up in Kinzel's timber, goin slow, watchin everything, or so I thought, an all of a sudden, jest a few feet away, there's Roy Edwards standin there lookin at me. I stopped dead in my tracks. Kind a scared me, ta tell the truth. He jest stood there lookin at me for a while, an then he sez, in that funny low voice, "Well, be careful. Don't hurt nobody." An then he walked away.

I went on a few steps an looked back an where was Roy? He was gone, disappeared. Didn't see'em when I'd come sneakin through the woods, couldn't see'em when I left. That was Roy Edwards.

It was white mittens that got'em. His kids usta come ta school with real nice homemade buckskin mittens. Story was that Roy's wife's mother made'em, Indian style, the tannin an all. An they were perty light colored. Whether Roy was wearin a pair a those homemade mittens on the day he was shot, I ain't sure. But he was wearin *white* mittens in deer season an some hunter thought the white mittens were a deer's tail, an he shot Roy Edwards dead. An that's the truth.

When I think about it, there were lots a shootings. Once George Eberhardt and John Edwards were out together on the Wisconsin River, in the winter, on the ice, an George had a .22 an somehow, fartin around, bein careless, George accidentally shot John in the chest. Didn't kill'em, but he could've.

An now I remember, out in Dakota, there were kids by the name a Kamel, an Harry Kamel was in my grade, an he had a couple a brothers, Tracy an Archie, an one or the other of'em shot Archie goin through a fence. Killed'em dead.

An Old Dave Ament killed a man hunting, an Pete Horgan shot Ned Fox in the hip.

Guns kin be wicked little things. Once that bullet's out a the barrel ya can't say "Stop, come back, it ain't what I intended." Too late fer that. Ya better know what yer intending before yer finger ever squeezes the trigger, an ya better know whether that patch a white over in the brush is a deer's tail or a man's white mittens. Somebody's gonna get hurt. Maybe somebody's gonna get killed. An then how ya gonna feel about *that* the rest a yer life? Not so good, I suspect.

Yer diggin kind a hard, Seedy. I kin remember a lot a stuff, an yer pesterin me with all these questions is causin me ta dig right down inta the froggy mud.

You gotta remember what it is *you* tell Birdy, sometimes, about "cutting the Old Man some slack." Maybe Birdy's been coachin *you*.

Let's turn the tables a little bit. Spoze I asked *you* what *you* were doin when *you* were fourteen, fifteen an sixteen, an me expectin *you* ta answer like you had it all down in a book.

Well, let me think a minute.

Deadhead Poverty PhD

Ya know, if ya think I'm gettin kind a aggravated with this whole business, well, I ain't. Well, maybe jest a little bit. Sometimes. But I been around long enuff ta know that what seems like aggravation kin be a kind of impatient excitement that bubbles up when somethin you forgot, or somethin you jest didn't think about fer years an years, is comin up out a the mud. Frogs an all.

So I ain't sayin no. I ain't callin it quits. I'm saying there's sometimes gotta be a delay between the question an the answer. An if ya think the answer's always gonna be clear or quick, well, yer mistaken. There's things I gotta dance around a little.

I'm doin the best I can, an that better be good enuff, cuz that's all yer gonna get. An I don't mean ta be mean about it. That's jest the way it is.

See, a lot a things I did after graduatin with that PhD in Poverty was preparin me ta be a lumberjack, ta work in the woods, an ta get perty damn good at it. That trainin started already when I was in school, when I had ta cut firewood with that dull old saw. An that didn't change when I got outa school.

We never had wood up for the winter. Now we do it different. Been times we've had wood up enuff for a couple a years. But not then. So, chances are when I got outa school I was back doin what, seems like, I'd always done. Cut wood with a dull saw for the cookstove an the heater stove.

But bein a big boy, outa school an livin close ta the landing, was what eased me inta lumberjackin. See, Old Dave Ament had got a gypo job cleanin out a patch a timber on the west bank a the Wisconsin River, jest above Grandfather Falls. An he hauled those logs down the Wisconsin River, in the winter, on the ice, an then up the Boulder to the landing. See, Kinzel had already pulled the rails in the area where that patch a timber was standin, an that meant usin the ice. But that route took'em inta our land an *acrost* our land, in order ta get to the landing.

In fact, when Old Dave was markin out his trail, from the Boulder an acrost our land, he had ta come up a little rise, an in the middle of his trail there was a rock stickin up an he couldn't dig it out so he decided ta blast it.

He did that by cappin it, twice, with dynamite. I was watchin. First time I was ever around blastin, not countin Mike Karban an his Fourth a July celebration. But it wasn't the last.

Now "cappin" meant he put a charge a dynamite *on top* a the rock, under a mud pack, before settin it off. He had ta do that twice before that rock was low enuff ta let the sleds pass over.

Dynamite those days was easy ta get. You jest went ta the hardware store an bought it. Later, I did that lots a times.

Those gypo jobs were left for a reason. The big loggin companies sized'em up an knew they'd be hard ta do. So they left'em for the little guys ta come in later an lose their asses on. An I think that's exactly what Old Dave Ament did. Lost his ass.

Now Dave didn't have enny trouble gettin big sled loads a logs *down* the Wisconsin, but he started ta have trouble getting'em *up* the Boulder, an he had *lots* a trouble gettin'em up an over our land. Horses kin do a lot a pullin, but they ain't caterpillars. They ain't machines. They're sweatin an steamin an breathin hard, an those sledloads a logs got smaller an smaller as those horses churned the snow up those last pulls. Teamsters had ta throw logs off the loads so the horses could make it, an there were logs layin everywhere. An those logs had ta be picked up, an that took time.

Now those gypo guys worked as short a men as they possibly could. An so Old Dave was always short a man at the landing, especially when it came time ta load logs onto the rail cars. An that's where I was handy help.

Dave'd come ta our place an ask if I'd come drive crosshaul team. An he always paid me somethin, an I was always willin ta go.

See, ya got rollways a logs, up on skids, layin as close ta the track as you could get'em. An then there was a contraption called a jammer, mounted on skids, so it could get pulled inta place beside the railroad cars.

Now in the big loggin outfits, like Kinzel or Rib Lake, that had their own rail line, the jammers were steam-powered outfits settin right *on* the tracks, hunkered up *over* the cars. But these gypo guys couldn't afford ennything like that. They were all tryin ta keep their butts from fallin off. So they worked short a men, an some of'em hired boys, like me. An that's where I learned the trade. Loadin, ennyway. Drivin crosshaul team. Pullin suckerlines. Canthook man. All a that.

Well, I never worked *on* the cars as a loaderman. I always worked on the ground, an I got good at it—though I usta wonder what'd happen ta me if somethin snapped when I was drivin the crosshaul team, walkin right behind the evener with tight lines, an those horses strainin an the cable tight as a fiddlestring runnin up through the jammer pulley ta the logs. Always danger. Or if one a the chains holdin the evener had let go, why it wudda snapped me in two, or broke my back.

I saw men get hurt, but not when I was workin for Old Dave, or for Harry Eberhardt an Old Pete Peterson. I usta drive crosshaul for them, too. Same sort a deal. Part-time, but only when they came an asked.

Ennything there was ta do on the ground loadin logs, well, I did it. I was big an quick an I saved damned near every nickle, until I had seventy-five dollars in the bank. An seventy-five dollars for a kid my age was a lot a money.

I was workin. An I was rich.

I guess that means I gotta tell ya more about Grampa Coster.

See, when we first came ta Wisconsin, we lived with Grampa an Gramma in their big brick house on South Foster Street. They'd come, I don't know, the previous summer or spring, somethin like that, but Aunt Minnie wasn't livin with'em ennymore by the time we arrived.

She'd flown the coop an gone back ta Ohio or Kentucky an she'd married a guy (don't ask me when), a guy named Jack Dixon. Sometime later—an I can't remember how long this was, either—Grampa an Gramma moved back ta Ohio or Kentucky, too, an they did it on account a Minnie.

Minnie an Jack wanted ta open a cafe or a restaurant, right near a ball park, an they persuaded Grampa an Gramma ta mortgage their land an house an loan'em the money in order ta open that cafe. They didn't *sell* the brick house, but they did *rent* it out. An they went down ta help, an they were gone several years.

Grampa got so he kind a detested Jack. Or so I heard. Story was he even went once ta buy a gun, with the intention a shootin Jack, but for some reason they wouldn't sell'em the gun. So things weren't all sweetness an light.

Well, I'm guessin here about the time. It cudda been spring or summer a '27, somethin like that, an Grampa comes back an he comes out ta Boulder an he's all dressed up real nice an he asks me, "Do you have seventy-five dollars?"

I'm wonderin how come he knows I got seventy-five dollars—my little brain is figgerin it out real fast—an I suspect my Ma had told'em.

An then he asks if he kin borrow it. When I tell'em it's in the bank, in a savings account, he sez, "Well, you kin jest sign that book an they'll let me have the money." That's what I did, an the bank gave'em the money. Grampa Coster got it.

An then he went back ta Ohio, or Kentucky, or wherever it was.

But he didn't take the money with'em. That brick house had developed a leaky roof when renters were in it, an Grampa had ta have it reshingled. Cost'em seventy-five dollars. Men from Wenzel Hardware did it.

Grampa said he'd pay me back, but he never did. But when I'd signed my savings book an given it to'em, he opened a little package a sweet cigars an we each had a smoke.

Now me an Jake Karban had made a little raft an put it on the Boulder. Jake smoked, an he'd share with me, us out on that raft. But if Pa got a wiff of it on me, he'd blister my ass. So I already had a taste for tobacco.

In fact, there was a family back in Dawson, name a Mayen, who had a ranch up north but owned a house in town where some a the family stayed during the school year, so the kids could go ta school. Too far ta come from the ranch everyday. An, like most places in Dawson, the house had a barn close by, an those Mayen boys'd go ta the barn an chew tobacco. Chew an spit, chew an spit.

Well, I had ta give it a try, too, but I couldn't take it. Made me sick.

But Grampa's sweet little cigar sure was good. Only cost me seventy-five dollars. Most expensive cigar I ever smoked.

Sayin "blister" an thinkin a Dawson reminds me of a girl named Abbey Lewis. Her Pa was deaf—us kids only knew'em as Old Man Lewis—an he was walkin down the railroad track after a real bad snowstorm an the train came up behind'em and killed'em.

But Abbey was Clara's an Mary's age, somewhere in there, an she had a pony she usta ride bareback. She'd come see my sisters, then jump on her pony an gallop away in a streak a dust. I never heard ennybody else ever call a horse "Blister," but that's what Abbey called hers. Blister.

Maybe that pony did ta her what my Pa did ta me.

I wonder if Abbey Lewis smoked cigars? Or if her Blister did?

Well, I told ya a little about how I got trained in lumberjackin, the classes I had ta take in school, an all that kind a crap, so I might as well tell ya about—how should I tell ya?—about the *correspondence courses* I took ta be a farmer. Same sort a advanced trainin in both, ya know.

Well, of the two, the deeper root is the farmin one, cuz that goes right back ta bein born, back ta Dawson, back ta livin in North Dakota. We always had cows an horses an chickens an sometimes turkeys, besides elephants an kangaroos an that kind a stuff. Kind a wild out there on the prairie.

An *prairie* is why the lumberjackin root doesn't go back so far. See, somebody'd cut all the prairie trees, years before I was born. Even the stumps were rotted an gone. Maybe the Indians did it fer tipi poles. An there wasn't no 'lectric stoves those days. Poor buggers had ta burn somethin ta cook their gopher meat. Big job cuttin down those prairie trees with little stone hatchets. Must a took'em years. But they did it.

Ennyway, if ya really want ta hear about how I got ta workin on a farm in Wisconsin, I got ta tell ya about Fred Schulz. But in order ta tell you about how I came ta know Fred Schulz well enuff ta work for'em, I got ta tell ya about a boat. Funny as that sounds, that's the way it is. This farmin story starts with a boat.

See, Harry Eberhardt lived next to the Wisconsin River, downstream from the mouth a the Boulder, less'n two miles from us. East, mostly, an a little south. An Harry had a boat. I jest loved that boat, an I wanted one, too. So I asked my Pa if he'd make me one, an he said he would, but I had ta come up with the lumber.

Now where the Wisconsin River comes curvin around the north end a the Sixth Ward, in Jensen, there was a sawmill run by a man named Ollhoff. An wherever else this man Ollhoff got his logs from I do not know, but I do know he bought lots a logs from guys who fished deadheads outa the river, mostly upstream from the sawmill.

I saw those guys lots a times, two men in a boat, with some kind a flotation arms stickin out both sides, lookin kinda like a giant water spider, ya know, both men standin up, never rowin, always polin, an they'd be lookin in the water an pokin around on the bottom, searchin fer deadheads.

Now what's a "deadhead"? Well, could be a son who—well, ferget about that. That wouldn't be nice ta say. Whether or not it might be true.

A deadhead's a sunken log. An there were lots a sunken logs in the Wisconsin River, especially in that area jest upstream from the Sixth Ward, cuz it was there the riverpigs usta sort logs an put'em in log corrals fer the different mills.

I'm talkin pine logs here, when they usta float'em down the river, an the men they called riverpigs were out walkin on those logs—corked shoes, a course—an herdin'em inta the right pen fer the different sawmills. See, all a those logs were marked with a markin hammer. They were marked before they were rolled in the water an floated down. But a course they got all tangled up, mixed together, as they came floatin down on their rubber rafts an swim fins. Sunglasses, ya know. Maybe a bottle a beer. Gettin a sun tan. Snorkles.

Ennyway, these guys in the waterspider boats'd be out there, pokin around, an when they found deadheads, they'd get'em up off the bottom with their pike poles an chain'em to their boats, an when they had all they could handle, they'd pole downstream ta Ollhoff's mill, an he'd buy'em. Buy deadheads from the waterspider fellas.

I bought five boards from Ollhoff's mill. I took'em home an Pa made me a boat. A twelve-footer. I spoze you could call it a deadhead boat. An when it was done, I dragged it to the Boulder an poled it down to the Wisconsin—had ta drag it over lots a riffles—an then on down ta Eberhardts'. I was really proud a that boat.

Now when Harry Eberhardt saw it, he jest stood there an laughed. See, most boats are peaked in the front, wide in the middle, an then they taper back a little to the back end. Makes'em kind a sleek an slippery in the water. But Pa'd been in a hurry, maybe, an he didn't bend those boards ta taper back from the middle, so it sort a looked like a homemade wooden snowplow, ya know, only with a bottom in it, or—what a ya call'em?—a *triangle*.

Harry laughed an laughed an then he sez, "An I thought yer Pa was a carpenter!" An he laughed some more.

Well, first I'd been proud a my boat an then, all of a sudden, I was hurt. Hard ta figger now whether I was hurt count a Harry laughin at my boat or laughin at my Pa. Some a both, maybe.

So I poled that deadhead snowplow back up the Boulder—had ta drag it over the same old riffles, a course, an it's always harder goin up than it is comin down—an where the two arms a the Boulder come together, I pulled it up out a the river, inta the brush, an I got some tools an tore the back end a that boat apart an I rebuilt it myself. When I was done it was tapered. It might not a been a perfessional job, exactly, but I had me a boat that looked like a boat an not like a snowplow. Or a deadhead *triangle*.

An now we're gettin up ta Fred Schulz.

I don't know what caused Fred ta drive inta our yard an ask about fishin. But he did. Pa wasn't too interested, but I was, an I took Fred down ta look at my boat an ta see that long hole in the river, jest downstream from where I rebuilt the snowplow.

Now by "fishin," Fred didn't mean sittin on the bank with a pole an a line waitin for a fish ta bite. Oh, no! Fred had a chickenwire net. An when he saw my boat an that long hole taperin to a riffles on the upstream end, right away he wanted ta put that net acrost the river on the upstream end a that hole. An that's exactly what we did.

Next mornin we came back an went out in my boat an lifted the net. Well, we had fish in the boat until the water was jest about comin in over the sides. Suckers, mostly. I think we kept some of 'em, but Fred took most of 'em. *Lots* a fish.

See, there's a couple stories in the Bible about boats almost sinkin becuz a all the netted fish, though I don't think they had chickenwire in those days. An somehow I don't think you know too much about the Bible, Seedy, cuz there ain't enny stories in there about game wardens walkin on the water.

Ennyway, next mornin Fred was back again, an we had fish, but they were fewer. Next mornin after that we went back again an that net was layin on the far bank, all cut ta pieces with a tin snips. Somebody'd found it. I don't think it was the game warden, cuz somebody wudda got pinched. I think somebody else was maybe nettin upstream an discovered there weren't enny fish comin up an went down ta try an figger out why.

Well, he figgered out why, alright, an there's Fred's net all chopped ta pieces, layin up on the bank. An that put a stop to our fishin.

That wudda been in the spring, ya know, cuz that's when the suckers are runnin.

Now I don't think I worked for Fred that summer—that cudda been the summer a '27—becuz I skidded spruce pulp for'em one winter before I helped'em on his farm. So it cudda been the summer a '28 I worked for'em on the farm, down on Joe Snow Road, maybe six, seven miles from home. Somethin like that. An I didn't work for'em over a month. I think I got two dollars a day, plus room an board.

Mrs. Schulz fed good. Her an Fred had a few cows an sold the cream ta the creamery. The skim milk they fed ta their pigs. So there was always meat on the table, lots a good smoked meat.

See, those old Dutchmen liked their smoked meat, an they were good at makin it. Usually one person in the family was the smoker, an they were particular. I kin remember, later, workin in Berndts' loggin camp an one of'em sayin, "Over there's a smoketree. We'll take that one home." That's what they called a standin dead hard maple—a "smoker." Or a smoketree. Didn't matter if it was a little punky. That's what they wanted, a hard maple smoketree. They were particular.

See, there was a pea cannin company in Jensen, an that company contracted with lots a farmers ta grow peas for cannin. Fred was one of'em, an so was his brother, who lived right acrost the road. First day on the job it's four o'clock in the mornin an I'm out in the field already loadin pea vines, by hand, with a pitchfork, onta a wagon. *Green* pea vines, an they were *heavy*. An we didn't quit till it was dark, pushin on toward nine o'clock. Fer two dollars a day plus room an board.

When I wasn't loadin peas I was doin somethin else jest as hard. Had ta follow right behind the horse-drawn mower as it cut the peas an, with the *handle* of a pitchfork, keep the pea vines from sprawlin onta the row that already had been cut, ta keep'em from gettin tangled together. Hour after hour a walkin behind the mower, always flippin vines off a what's creepin up the mowboard.

An when I wasn't doin that I was up in the hay mow, mowin away loads a fresh hay that got dumped up there off a harpoon hook. Hot. Sweat. Work. Man, oh, man!

I think it was, maybe, a Sunday night, after a day at home during that month a workin for Fred, an Mrs. Schulz was in the kitchen bottlin up a batch a home brew out of a real big crock. An sitting there on chairs was Fred an two of his drinkin pals from up on Frostbite Avenue, Reinhold Kleinschmidt an Harry Krause. An they were ladling their cups full a that raw home brew, an they had all they could do ta keep from fallin off their chairs. They were *so* drunk.

Well, nobody called Reinhold Kleinschmidt "Reinhold." Everybody knew'em as *Bruder Langsam*, which means "Brother Slow." An he *was* slow, except sittin there in that kitchen, suckin up home brew, he was about as ready ta fall off his chair as fast as enny man alive. An Fred was sittin there laughin.

Seems like Fred kind a liked ta get people drunk. When I skidded spruce pulp for'em the previous winter—that was Fred's pulpin job about a mile west a where Batchelders lived, an Fred stayed in Old Man Karban's shack, cuz nobody was livin there jest then—an Fred invited me over to the shack on my birthday. I wudda been, what?, sixteen, seventeen, somethin like that. An he opened up a quart of his wife's home brew an he gave it ta me ta drink. An I did.

Well, I made it home, kind a staggerin, an my Ma was madder'n a wet hen. She didn't like that trick *at all.*

But at Fred's farm I had ta get up real early ta go feed horses. Two teams. Mrs. Schulz would wake me. An one mornin I got up late. I don't know why. Maybe I jest overslept. Maybe Mrs. Schulz didn't wake me quite as early. I can't remember. But as I was walkin to the barn, Fred met me comin back. He'd already fed the horses. An he stood there an bawled me out real bad fer not doin my job.

Well, after breakfast I had ta go get a load a cookstove wood, back of a field, with Fred's old Model T pickup. An Mrs. Schulz came along. I told'er I was gonna quit, an she asked me why. "Becuz Fred bawled me out so bad," I told'er.

Well, she must a told Fred at lunch cuz in the afternoon he gave me a real easy job, changin boxes on the pea viner. I figgered he was maybe tryin ta make up, ya know, for snappin at me, but I'd made up my mind. After supper I told'em I was quittin, an I walked home. The work was hard enuff without gettin bawled out besides.

Now I did work fer other guys on occasion, too. I'd help Mike Stevens fill silo two, three days, ya know, throwin corn bundles all day long. Usually didn't get paid nothin except for meals.

One year Clara an me worked about a week for Long Pete Peterson, acrost the Wisconsin River. He'd come up from farther south in Wisconsin an he always tried ta raise what he called a "cash crop." Sometimes that was potatoes. He had a mechanical potato digger, but Clara an me had the job a goin down the dug rows fillin bushel boxes with potatoes.

Clara was quicker'n me, an she'd be done with her row before I was done with mine, so she'd come help me. I couldn't keep up with her. An that work ain't easy, either. Not heavy, exactly, but yer bendin over all the time an perty soon ya feel like yer back is gonna break in two.

See, Long Pete had customers in town, an he'd load up his car an trailer with bushel boxes a potatoes an then deliver'em. On a wet day, a rainy day, I went along with'em—didn't get paid nothin, but it was somethin ta do—but Long Pete had ta stop on the way home an wet his whistle, an he had, maybe, one or two too many, cuz he drove like hell with this goofy grin on his face an damned near rammed that car right through the back end a his garage.

We called'em "Long" Pete cuz he was such a tall man. Same fella who got drunk an his wife pushed'em out a the rowboat—but I told ya that one, too, already. Maybe we should a called'em Hand-Paddlin Pete, I don't know.

But we ain't done with this correspondence course jest yet. Still got a couple a more examinations ta take.

See, I helped Pa an Ma make hay all the time. Some a that was done in meadows next ta old loggin camps—Camp 30, Camp 25. Such as that. But we also made hay up on the old Anderson Homestead, up off a Frostbite Avenue, past where Harry Krause an Bruder Langsam lived.

Grampa Coster had a one-horse mower, an when the hay was dry up there on the Anderson place, I'd bunch it with a dump rake pulled behind Grampa's white horse. Grampa called'em Dick. We loaded the wagon by hand, with pitchforks, an that hay got stored in the old log barn right there on the Homestead. We didn't have enny place ta put it at home, an in the winter I'd come up with our horse, Old Jack, an haul some hay home on a sled. That's how we lived.

But one day I was out there rakin hay with Dick an there's Grampa Coster creepin acrost the field with his shotgun, held like he meant to shoot something, headed for a deer lick that was jest on the edge a the brush. So I sez "Whoa" ta Dick, kind a quiet like, an I jest sat there on the seat a that dump rake, an Dick's standin there switchin flies, an if I look jest right I kin make out a deer in the lick. An Grampa's creepin closer an closer, hunkered down, ya know, sneakin, an all of a sudden he raises up an shoots an down goes that deer.

I think that was the first deer I ever saw shot. An Grampa Coster is the one that got'em, right there in the lick at the edge a Anderson Homestead.

Farmin wasn't all that far from huntin in those days. Things were still perty small an homemade an—what a ya call it?—*subsistence*. That deer meant meat on the table, an we were poor, an we were *hungry*.

Grampa got that deer. I was sittin there with Dick, watchin.

Well, here's one that might tickle yer funnybone. It's maybe about farmin. Or farm work, ennyway. Hayin. An it's got a parrot in it. An some "sauerkraut."

See, when Grampa Coster was around, I always had ta go down an help'em make hay on his land off a South Foster Street, right next ta Devil's Crick. This was kind of a yes-no proposition fer me becuz the work was real hard, an I was jest a kid, but I really loved my Grampa Coster.

I think I wudda fallen over dead for'em, if I'd had to. So I *didn't* want ta go but I *did* want ta go. I *had* ta go ennyway, so it didn't matter much what I *wanted*. Usually took us most of a week ta make his hay.

Kitty-corner acrost Devil's Crick was a tavern run by a older man name of August Smite. I think I first got ta know him when Gramma would give me a nickle or a dime an have me run over ta August Smite's ta buy Grampa a pouch a tobacco.

Now sometimes Grampa liked ta go over an have a beer at Smite's, an so him an August were kind a friends. An when we were done makin hay at Grampa's, we went an did the same fer August Smite. Made hay. Usually only a couple a loads, but fer a kid that's already tuckered out, a couple a loads seems like more'n yer ever gonna get done.

But a course we did get done. An Old Smite would give me a quarter or a half a dollar. That was nice.

August Smite had a car, but he kept that car in a garage an had a tarp over it an he hardly ever drove it. What he mostly drove was a horse an buggy. That's what he almost always took when he had ta go inta town. Wasn't all that far, but that's what he did. An that's why he needed the hay. The horse ate most of it. The buggy only got a little.

I been kind a holdin off on this parrot business. See, August Smite had two of'em, two parrots, an one of'em could talk. An every time Grampa an me walked inta that tavern that parrot would squawk out, "This man wants some sauerkraut."

August Smite had taught'em ta say that becuz booze was illegal an he wasn't spozed ta be sellin ennything except what they called "near beer," which was one-half a one percent, or somethin like that. Weak stuff. But all taverns sold the real stuff, too. Served it, sold it, but they had ta be careful. So you wouldn't want yer parrot callin out, "This man wants some booze," or "This man wants some moonshine." That wouldn't've worked at all.

"This man wants some sauerkraut" worked good enuff. Only this was the kind a fermented cabbage ya had ta drink.

But it's too damned bad when a man can't even trust his own parrot. Kind a makes ya wonder what the world's comin to.

4

Ends Too Short To Use

Some time I'll tell ya about gettin buck fever, which is a real aggravatin thing that kin come over you as yer tryin ta shoot a deer. It makes ya kind a crazy an jumpy, an the gun won't hold still, an mostly ya miss an then, when it's over, ya feel real stupid an mad at yerself. I had a real dose a that for quite a while.

This pickin an choosin a stories isn't exactly like buck fever, though. Maybe it's more like gettin lost in the woods an there's a bunch a trails ya *could* go down but ya don't know which one ta take, so ya start feelin kind a swamped an confused.

But I guess it's like ennything else—ya jest got ta start somewhere, even if, with this story-tellin business, it seems like every time ya start yer startin all over again from scratch. I think some a this feelin comes from wantin ta do it right. An then I think, "Well, Hank, what do ya mean by 'right'?" An I guess I mean tryin ta tell it about as clear as I kin remember it, tryin ta get you ta *see* it the way I kin see it in my mind. Jest like it was yesterday. Jest the way it happened.

I think yer gonna get sick a hearin "jest like it was yesterday." But there probably ain't a lot a "tomorrow" left fer me. An since I got me a huge big stack a "yesterday," it's what I got ta share. So jest try'n put up with it.

Well, some things got dropped, an I gotta go back an pick'em up. Like tellin about skiddin spruce pulp fer Old Fred Schulz. But we'll jest let that one lay there a while cuz I'd rather tell ya a couple more stories that involve my deadhead boat.

If *you* had a choice between skiddin spruce pulp in the cold winter behind a half-blind horse or goin fishin, what'd you choose? That'd be a no-brainer, as the kids seem ta like ta say.

Ennyway, Grampa Coster told me he'd never caught a fish with a fish pole. Never. Not one. Said he'd caught lots a fish runnin trotlines, maybe in the Ohio River, I don't know, but he'd never monkeyed around with a fish pole. He wanted ta catch a fish with a fish pole. An he wanted me ta take him fishin. He wanted ta go in my boat, an he wanted me ta take'em down to the mouth a the Boulder.

So I did. I took'em, though I don't think he knew what he was askin. See, it's—what?—a good crooked mile from where I had the boat pulled up in the brush down to the mouth, an that stretch a water is chock-full a riffles. Oh, it's got pools in it, but each pool's got a riffles at each end, an there's lots a places ya gotta use yer imagination ta see ennything resemblin a "pool." Nothin but steps a riffles, lots an lots a rocks.

I got'em down there, alright, an I got'em back. We were gone all day. We fished an fished in the deeper water at the mouth, but Grampa never even got a bite. Not one single stinkin bite.

An then I had ta pole an pull'em back up. He was a old man, an he never once got out a the boat ta help. So I not only had ta pull the boat over the riffles, I had ta pull the boat over the riffles with Grampa Coster sittin in it.

I was one tired fella when we got back. I think skiddin spruce pulp would've been a whole lot easier.

Another time—it was spring, but the water was low for spring—I happened ta notice suckers runnin up the riffles. So I got my little brother John, an he was jest a little kid, got'em ta sit in the front a the boat, an I poled it to the top of a riffle, tied the front to a big rock in the river, let the butt end a the boat swing down, an I stood in the back with my fish spear, waitin for the fish.

Now those fish seemed ta be like deer in that they had their trails, their paths, an they seemed ta come up the riffles like it was all marked out for'em. Turn right, turn left, stop here an wait for the light ta turn green. Traffic cops. Crossing guards. All that sort a thing.

John was sittin in the front fer ballast, ya might say, an I was standin in the back, watchin real close, with the business end a the fish spear *in the water*.

See, when ya jab at a fish ya can't have that spear way up in the air an think yer gonna get'em, cuz you ain't. Fish are fast, an if that spear makes a splash, well, you might as well forget it becuz that fish ain't gonna be there ta get jabbed. So you hold that spear *in the water*, an yer watchin an yer waitin an yer *ready*.

Well, I speared a mess a fish that day, an when it was enuff for a meal or two, I poled us back to the spot in the brush where I always pulled the boat out a the water. I pushed us up to the bank, between a couple a clumps a alder brush, an there was a man, a total stranger, standin there waitin.

I was real scared, but there wasn't no such a thing as runnin away. There's John, there's the boat, there's the fish, there's me. An there's the spear. An there's that man standin there waitin.

"Don't you know," he sez, "it's illegal to spear fish in a trout stream." He didn't mean it as a question.

I don't think I said ennything. There wasn't nothin ta say.

An then he bends down an looks real careful at the fish, an he sez, "Well, you've only got suckers. You take'em home. But you ought to know that the game warden is just down the river a little ways."

There wasn't nothin ta do but take those fish an go. Ain't no "catch an release" with spearin. I think we cleaned those fish not knowin if the game warden was gonna show up an arrest us, but nobody ever came. We cleaned'em an we ate'em, jest like we always did.

I think that man jest might've been the game warden. But we were poor, an he probably knew it. This might've been the first time I started ta realize that game wardens could also let ya alone, if there was reason enuff for'em ta let ya be. Eight, nine kids livin in a tarpaper shack might a been reason enuff in those days. Maybe even a "no-brainer," as the kids like ta say— though there's always people who think the rules gotta be followed, even if it kills ya.

But that game warden, if that's what he was, bent the rules that day. I know a couple more instances where the rules got bent. Some day I'll tell ya what they were.

The priest from the Catholic church in Jensen usta come out sometimes an give instructions ta the older girls—Mary, Clara, an I spoze Daisy. Not me. I'd see'em comin, an I'd be out the door, hidin in the brush. They'd call an call, but little Henry wasn't nowhere ta be found.

Oh, I could hear'em, alright, but there was no way I was comin in. I wanted nothin ta do with that crap.

Sometimes the priest'd bring along a couple sacks a groceries. Once we pulled a couple boxes a corn flakes outa one a those sacks. What's this? What's "corn flakes"?

We tried'em, but that wasn't enny food for us. We needed somethin ta *eat*. Corn flakes were a big joke.

Bruder Langsam an Harry Krause were clean-shaven men. Bruder was a average-sized man, but Harry was kinda short. They liked ta fish.

The first memory I got of'em was a spring soon after we'd moved inta the bunkhouse. Cudda been the spring a '23. An they had a old Model T. It was early in the mornin an they drove inta our yard an gave us a batch a suckers.

I don't know that I thought about it then, but later I figgered they'd been nettin'em.

All I knew was that they were trappers an hunters. I know Harry told me him an Bruder shot beaver in that big beaver pond acrost Frostbite Avenue from their log shack. Bruder was tight-lipped. He didn't say much. You couldn't learn nothin from Bruder. But Harry'd talk a little, an so you could get a glimpse inta how they lived.

Somehow they'd got this idea ta fence in that little lake—jest a pond, really—on their forty. The idea was muskrats. They were gonna fence in the muskrats an have'em as a steady source a furs. But that little lake is a bog lake. Ain't no cattails in it. An muskrats gotta have cattails. That's what they live on. They eat the roots.

So Harry an Bruder fenced it in—big job—but that didn't work. It couldn't work. It was a stupid idea. It was poor thinkin. I don't know if they saw a few muskrats in there, if that's what got'em goin on that hare-brained idea, or if they had in mind ta build the fence an then put in some breedin stock.

See, those were the years when raisin critters for fur was goin big. Fromm brothers, jest down in Marathon County, were gettin rich—so everybody said—on foxes. Silver-blacks they called'em. Hunnerds a dollars for a single pelt. So everybody was gonna get rich on fur.

Fourteen, fifteen, sixteen years old an I was pokin around in the brush all the time, everywhere, gettin ta know the country. Once I was comin up toward Harry an Bruder's place, through the woods, comin in from the southwest, in what would now be Steve Schulz's land—that's Old Fred's grandson—an I ran acrost a horse's head surrounded by wolf traps.

That was Bruder an Harry's work.

I ain't sure what caused'em ta want ta sell out, but they did. This cudda been '28, '29, somethin like that. An I somehow knew these two brothers, from Wausau, Joe an John Eiden, an they were popcorn men, both of'em bachelors who made their livin from popcorn wagons. An these brothers had got the silver fox bug. They thought they were gonna make a lot a money. But they needed some woods land. So I lined'em up with Harry an Bruder, an they bought that land. I thought I'd get a few bucks outa that, ya know, kind of a commission deal, but they never paid me ennything.

So Joe an John bought Harry an Bruder's forty, an they bought maybe a dozen pair a silver-blacks for breeding. A course then they had ta pen'em an feed'em. I know I helped'em cut ice on that little bog lake an put it in their little ice house, an then we went ta some farmer's place ta buy a couple a old plug horses ta feed the foxes. An that farmer wouldn't let the Eiden brothers buy those old horses unless they agreed ta butcher'em right there on the farm. I spoze that farmer didn't trust those guys not ta try an sell'em for work horses if they took'em off alive. They were old plugs.

So all one day I helped'em butcher those two horses, an the meat went inta the ice house.

But it wasn't long an the bottom went right outa the fur business. I was up at Eidens' quite a bit, helpin'em cut wood, that sort a stuff, an they didn't pay ennything, but the older brother, Joe, was a wonderful cook an he fed good, an he always invited me ta eat with'em. I think those were the best meals I ever had in those years.

An, in my pokin around—I was tryin, ya know, ta be a deer hunter, but I'd always get the buck fever— I knew a swamp northwest a Old Doc Sievert's place on the Boulder (a course, Old Doc wasn't in there yet), an that swamp was jest loaded with snowshoe rabbits. When Joe Eiden heard about that, he wanted me ta take'em up there. Gave me a shotgun ta use an a whole lot a shells, an off we went.

All I did was shoot rabbits. We came back through the woods together as far as Kelly Crick before we went our separate ways home. I gave'em back his shotgun, an you couldn't hardly see ennything a that man, cept for his head, he was so loaded down with strings a rabbits. He was like a fur man, nearly as wide as he was tall.

By then, I think, the prices had dropped an they couldn't afford horse meat ennymore. That's why Joe wanted rabbits. I even heard of a guy who turned his mink loose, after he'd had'em penned, becuz he couldn't afford ta feed' em. That's how bad it got.

I kinda lost track a Bruder Langsam an Harry Krause. Well, I knew Harry was also workin in Kinzel's camp, in the early '30s, same time as I was there, but we didn't work together, an that's all I knew. I don't think Bruder ever got married, but Harry did. He married a woman with four, five, six kids, an that didn't last long. I don't think Harry was prepared ta support a family. He was too usta eke out a livin in his own way, an then he'd drink up what he'd eked. Plus, by then it got ta be Depression, an wages were real low, if ya could find a job. So that didn't work fer Harry.

Well, Seedy, I spoze I kin tell ya this now. Yer sixty years old. You should be old enuff ta handle it. See, Harry Krause was kinda like yer grandfather. I mean, it was yer Gramma, yer mother's mother, who married Harry Krause.

You know it was yer Grampa Berndt that died in—what was it?—1930 or thereabouts. He ran that tavern in the Town a Corning, kitty-corner from where your Ma's buried in St. Paul's cemetery. Story was he drank up whatever profits he made, an that's what killed'em. Died a perty young man. But old enuff ta have five, six kids. An yer Gramma turned around an married Harry Krause. But Harry Krause wasn't enny sort of husband an he wasn't enny father ta all those kids. He didn't know ennything about supportin a family. So that didn't last long, at all. Big disaster.

So Harry is, an he ain't, yer Grampa, too.

I see this kinda shocks you, Seedy, but ya gotta get it outa yer head that all these stories don't have ennything ta do with *you*. I mean, they may be *my* stories, but like I tried ta tell ya early on, a lot a these stories ain't about *me*. Or they're only in part about me.

It's like walkin inta that rabbit swamp with Joe Eiden. Tracks everywhere. An sometimes one a those rabbits might sneak up behind and grab ya on the seat a yer pants.

Looks ta me like that's the way this rabbit's got you, Seedy. Right on the seat a yer pants.

We usta laugh at August Smite. Once in a while he'd pull the tarp off his car an drive it ta town. What we laughed at was he never shifted that car outa low gear. He'd be goin down the road, both hands grippin the steerin wheel, real focused, ya know, on *drivin*, an that car was jest crawlin along, about as fast as a person could walk.

A course I was a kid, an kids know all about everything. They think it's funny if some old guy is scared when he's drivin a machine that's brand new to'em, a thing that's got no ears an ain't gonna respond ta "whoa" and "giddy-up." Put me in front of a computer, an I'd be dumber'n August Smite behind the wheel. I wouldn't know giddy-up from whoa.

An that makes me think a my Pa.

Somewhere in '27, '28, somethin like that—I wudda been fifteen or sixteen—Pa'd actually got a little money ahead fer once, so he decided ta buy a little truck. So him an me went ta town, to a garage run by a couple a fellas name of Allen an Zander, right east a where the movie house sits now. An the cripple Pa had his eye on was a old Model T pickup with a little box on the back, an he bought it.

Well, he got it started alright, but he couldn't get it ta move. So the garage fellas took a look at it an said one a the clutch bands was wore out. So we had ta go home without it.

A few days later I went down ta get it. They'd put a new band in the transmission, an it would move. Now I wasn't too confident about drivin. I'd got ta drive Harry Eberhardt's car a couple a times when George'd take me along fer a ride. So I knew about turnin the steerin wheel an a little bit about shiftin an that sort a thing, but not much. (I don't think Pa'd ever driven a car in his life. Maybe that's why I got ta go down all by myself that second trip. I don't know.)

Ennyway, I didn't want ta drive outa town the main way—Jensen, ya know, is kinda strung out along the Wisconsin River, on a east-west line, an there'd a been over a mile a town ta drive through—so I went acrost the narrow bridge that points down toward Wausau an turned west on the sandy road that ran through Tannery Town. Not many people livin there.

I imagine now if I cudda seen myself grippin the steerin wheel an creepin down that sandy road I might a looked a lot like August Smite. An I might not a laughed so loud.

Ennyway, the route I took put me on South Foster Street, so I pulled inta Grampa Coster's yard. When he saw I was all by myself, he sez, "You ain't goin home by yerself. I'm comin with you." An he did. I don't think he thought I was a good enuff driver ta make it on my own.

But we made it. There were three pedals on the floor—I spoze I could tell ya I *pedalled* that truck all the way home—an one was for the clutch an low gear, one was for reverse, an one was for high gear an the brake. No stick shift. Ya had ta do all the shiftin, all the startin an stoppin, with yer feet.

Now this was before ya had ta have a driver's license. Nobody had such a thing. If you owned a car, you could drive it. I think it was later in the twenties when ya had ta have a license. First one I got cost me a quarter. Had ta fill out a form an send it in with twenty-five cents. A week or so later ya got yer license in the mail.

So we got Pa's truck home alright, but it didn't run good. Harry Eberhardt helped Pa fix it up so it ran better. In those days ya had ta be a mechanic if ya wanted ta drive a car. Pa wasn't enny mechanic. An that old truck was a junker, ennyway. Still, we got ta drive it quite a bit before it jest sat in the weeds an watched the world go by.

I don't remember how Grampa Coster got home.

Before Pa built me that deadhead snowplow, that triangle speedboat, my Ma wanted ta go fishin. So she'n Pa'n me borrowed Harry Eberhardt's boat, an I rowed the three of us upstream on the Wisconsin to the mouth a the Boulder. An we sat there an fished.

Ends Too Short To Use 69

Ma'd never fished before, not with a hook'n line, ennyway. Well, she'd helped plenty when we'd go nettin with chickenwire in the Boulder. But she'd never caught a fish on a line.

So we were fishin there with bait'n bobbers, ya know, an Ma gets a big bite. Her bobber goes down an stays down. Well, she didn't know ennything about settin the hook, about givin it a good jerk, so she jest tugs kinda gentle on that line an this monster fish sticks his front end outa the water an shakes itself free a Ma's hook.

Weeks later an she's still talking about seein that big fish spit her hook out. Jest like it was yesterday.

Some a these stories are so little they ain't hardly big enuff ta get told. Kinda like the old spinster lady that died an when they went ta clean out her house everything was boxed neat an nice, an one box was full a little bitty pieces a string, all packed up so neat, an the label said "Ends Too Short Ta Use."

I think some a these stories are ends too short ta use.

For instance, I'm jest sittin here thinkin about the trail that usta run east a the Anderson Homestead, all the way down to the Wisconsin River. About two miles, maybe. South a that trail it'd been logged. Brush an small trees comin back. But north a the trail it was timber. I took my Pa's single-shot .22 an walked down that trail to the river. Jest pokin along, ya know, takin my time, but also watchin.

An somewheres along that trail I saw a partridge on the ground an I shot it. Now by the time I got ta the river, I was hungry. When a kid's hungry, he's *hungry*. He wants somethin ta eat an he wants it *now*.

So I built a little fire an cleaned that bird the best I could, tried ta make somethin ta hold it out of the fire while it roasted, all a that with the big Wisconsin rollin close by. Kind of a hobo thing, ya know, free'n easy livin. Runnin water right at hand to wash up in. Take a bath, if I wanted to.

Not too bad if you like yer meat—an meat *only*—half raw an without enny salt.

I think the hobo life is kinda—what a ya call it?—*romantic* if yer lookin at it from the outside. From the inside it makes you perty grateful fer sittin down at yer Ma's table. At least the meat is cooked, even if you do have ta wash the dishes afterwards.

There's a lot a stories gonna come now, Seedy, sort a like cows all tryin ta squeeze through the barn door at the same time, though some of 'em are gonna have a hard time getting their heads in the right stanchion.

I keep tryin ta tell ya these memories ain't all lined up in alphabetical order, short ta tall, young ta old, dumb ta smart, each of 'em with a number ta call out when it's their turn. Yer getting'em as yer getting'em, what else kin I say?

I don't know who ya think yer doin this for—fer you an yer brothers? fer all the grandkids? jest fer the hell of it? But it's kinda perkin me up a bit. It's kinda fun ta see what's coming up outa the mud. Most a the time, ennyway. Offen enuff. Some a the frogs might have teeth, so ya better watch out.

I think, maybe, jest ta keep the cows from goin too wild, I'll tell ya two stories that are pointed up Frostbite Avenue. Ain't no use spookin the cows jest fer the hell of it. Enuff chasin as it is.

Ennyway, I'm gonna tell ya about gettin ta know Al Briest. But there's some dynamite in that story, so I better tell ya about Tony Zillman first.

Tony was a older man, a single man an somethin of a loner. He lived with his brother-in-law, name a Ed Wanless. I knew Tony since I was in the young teens an usta go to the house parties that were held here an there. Once a month or so in the summer. Victrola playin. Women an kids dancin inside. Men outside suckin on moonshine.

But Tony never had much ta do with the men an their drinkin. He'd show up at the parties, but he'd kinda hang out with us older kids, an he'd sing us little ditties. He paid attention to us kids, an we liked that. So I had this perty good feelin about Tony Zillman.

See, those years everybody knew everybody, not like now. I mean, we got neighbors now an we never even been in their houses. An they ain't been in ours. But that's not how it was back then. Somebody'd move inta the neighborhood an everybody would come ta see ya, come ta visit, wantin ta know who ya are. An it didn't end there, either. More'n likely you'd find somethin ta do together. Cut wood, maybe, or help build somethin or, for the women, makin quilts. Some a that was puttin yer nose inta everybody else's business, cuz there was always gossip, but there was real helpin each other, too, an that's how some a the bigger things got done, like buildin a house. Folks jest pitched in an got'er done.

Ennyway, the town had some money ta spend on improvin the south end a Frostbite Avenue. Tony Zillman's brother-in-law, Ed Wanless, was on the town board, an Ed was the road boss. Tony was the dynamite man.

Frostbite Avenue went north, alright, but it was jest a rutted trail that dodged around big rocks an stumps, an this road crew was spozed ta make a road outa that mess. There were five, six men an two teams a horses, an I was the youngest a the lot, jest a big kid really, sixteen, maybe seventeen years old. Somethin like that.

All I did that first mornin was throw brush an hunks a stumps from Tony's blastin, an roll rocks. At lunch time we're sittin on rocks an stumps, eatin our sandwiches while the horses are eatin their oats an hay, an Tony sez ta Ed, "I can't stay far enuff ahead a you guys. Everytime I blast a couple a stumps, the men gotta clear out. I gotta have some help."

Well, Ed thinks about that a while an then he starts goin down the line a men, startin with the oldest. "Will you help Tony?" An everybody sez no. Nobody wants ta have ennything ta do with dynamite.

Well, I'm the youngest of the crew, jest a big kid, but I see how it's goin, everybody sayin no ta Ed, an my little brain is thinking, "Tony don't get hurt. If Tony don't get hurt, why would I get hurt?"

So perty soon it's my turn ta answer. An Ed sez, "What about you, Huntz?" Or Heini or Hank or whatever he called me. I had lots a nicknames those days. Everybody's lookin at me an I sez, "Sure. I'll work with Tony."

So after lunch Tony took me aside an taught me how ta use dynamite. He was a man a few words. He sez ta me real serious, "There's one main rule. An that is ya gotta keep yer mind on what yer doin. One mistake with this stuff"—he was holdin a stick a dynamite in his hands—"an it might jest be yer last." That's how I got my PhD in dynamite. An then we went ta work.

First he had me watch'em a couple a times, ta see how he stuck the dynamite under the stumps, a couple sticks at a time, not too far apart, how ta set the cap'n fuse, how ta hold the match, how ta hold yer striker rock, which charge ta light first, where ta go ta get outa the way a the blast. An then he watched me real close as I did it.

Well, it ain't long an Tony an me are a real team, each of us blastin three stumps at a crack, an we left the rest a the crew behind. We did that for over two weeks, till the money ran out, I guess, but by then I'd kinda learned the trade. I got ta be a dynamite man, jest like Tony.

Well, not quite. At the very end a the job we came back to the south end a Frostbite Avenue an there, buttin in from the east, is Mail Route Road, an there's a long low spot, jest a alder swamp really, an Tony's got ta blast a ditch on the north side. But he sez ta me, "This one needs stronger stuff an you can't help me."

I didn't get paid for that last half-day, cuz I wasn't doin ennything, but I jest had ta stay an watch Tony make that ditch. He did it in two long shots. Took'em quite a while ta poke those sticks a strong dynamite in the muck, but when he set'em off an the mud had settled he had a nice clean ditch runnin all the way from Frostbite to that little crick on the east side a that alder swamp.

That's how I learned ta shoot dynamite. From Tony Zillman. On Frostbite Avenue.

Now Tony was the elected assessor for the Town. An some years later somebody asked me ta run against Tony for the job, an I did, an I beat'em. But at the Board a Review there were men who'd come ta challenge my assessment of their "personal property," cows'n sheep mostly, an the town board sided with the fellas who challenged me, an I figgered all along they were lyin.

So I never ran again. Too much shady dealin. Too much cheatin.

Now Al Briest wasn't a real important person in my life, but it's Al's Pa who bought the old Anderson Homestead an, if nothin else, that put a end to our makin hay up there.

Story was that Al's Pa was a Lutheran minister from South Dakota, an Al was spozed ta make a farm outa the Homestead. But Al was a barber. He wasn't a farmer. He gave it a try, though it didn't last long.

We got ta know the family right away, cuz on the very day Al an his wife an their little girl came, they got stuck on Karban Hill, or at least their Model T got stalled an the trailer that was hooked on behind jackknifed in the road, an so me'n Pa went over ta see what we could do. Turns out they'd rented Old Man Karban's shack for a while, so when we got'em straightened out, they didn't have far ta go.

An while they were stayin at Karban's place, Pa was visitin his deer lick down by the river an a deer came in an he shot it. Well, Al wanted ta know what that shot was about, an next thing he knew we brought'em a hunk a venison. An then Al wanted ta get a deer himself. He had a shotgun. So him an me went up ta the Homestead, up in the old log barn, an looked out the window toward that same lick where Grampa Coster had shot his deer, an, by golly, a deer came in an Al shot it right outa the barn window.

That old log house up there wasn't hardly fit ta live in ennymore, so my Pa helped Al build the house that's still standin. There was a thicket a balsam trees between the new house an the road an Al didn't like'em there, so he cut'em all down. Maybe he was proud of his new house an wanted everybody ta see it, I don't know. But those trees grew right back, an it's as thick now as when Al Briest cut'em down.

Al got a team a little horses an he bought a hand plow an tried ta do some plowin. But he didn't know how. Plus he'd bought too big a plow for those horses, an the little brutes had a hell of a time pullin it. So I helped'em, an we got'er licked.

Now the bottom end a that field was close ta Kelly Crick, an it wasn't long an the beavers had a dam big enuff acrost the crick ta flood a piece a the field. An Al got perty upset.

"Well," I sez, "I know how ta fix that," an we somehow got us a few sticks a dynamite an I blew a couple a holes in that beaver dam. Big joke. Next mornin that dam was all fixed. So I sez ta Al, "Let's give'em some more," an I set off a bigger blast that at least kept'em busy quite a while. But beavers aren't quitters, an there ain't no stoppin'em unless ya kin trap'em out. At that point I didn't know ennything about trappin beaver. That came later.

A relative a Al's came from somewhere an the two of'em wanted me ta take'em to a deer lick way up by Camp 24, way off a what's now Boulder Road, an so I did. Or maybe they took me. I was still jest a big kid. But they had a gallon jug a red wine along, an that wasn't so smart.

Perty soon those guys are drunker'n skunks, an then the jug got dropped. But only the top broke out, an most a the wine was still in it. Or some of it was. Then they had a discussion about whether it was safe ta drink the wine that was left in the jug, count a all the broken glass that was in there. Well, they had no way a filterin the wine, but they weren't about ta waste it, either, so real careful like they drank the rest a the wine out a that jug with the broken glass in it.

I don't think I need ta tell ya we didn't get enny deer. Not that night.

Here's a really little one. The smallest cow comes in the barn last.

One evenin this carload a guys shows up from Wausau. One of 'em I knew, but jest barely. They had a big, old car, four doors, seats in front an back, four, five guys. They had a gun an wanted ta go shine deer.

"Come along," they sez. "You kin show us where ta go."

So I got in an we went up past Batchelders', headed west an north, up those set a steps on the country road. The driver had the lights on, goin slow. No deer. No deer. No deer. An perty soon the expectation a seein deer starts ta peter out.

But the road was full a snowshoe rabbits. So we turned around an started ta come back. We were jest north a Wolf Crick, in there somewheres, an one a the guys sez, "Let's catch some rabbits."

I spoze grownup people wouldn't a done it, but they dug out a couple a old raincoats an two of us got out on the running boards, one on each side—I was one of 'em—an the driver jest crept along an we'd dive off an flop on top a the rabbit, or try to, but we never got one—close, maybe, but the rabbit always manage ta scoot away.

An laugh! I think that car had all the laughs it could handle.

I was one a the guys holdin a raincoat an doin bellyflops on top a those rabbits. Or where the rabbit was spozed ta be. Skinned-up knuckles an dirt on our faces. But we had fun even though every stinkin rabbit got away. Lots a fun—huntin rabbits with raincoats.

I kin sense yer wantin ta get to that winter when I skidded spruce pulp for Fred Schulz, Seedy, kind a unfinished business, but yer old enuff ta know life's full a unfinished business, an maybe some of it never does get done.

I ain't tryin ta put ya off jest for the fun of it. It jest seems ta me that we'd better get around the neighborhood a little bit first, cuz I have the feelin that once we get ta the lumberjackin stuff we're gonna be there a while. Maybe not. I been wrong before. But I spoze that's news ta you.

I kin think a three things ta touch on, for sure, before we go to the woods. One is Orin Sommers tryin ta farm. Another is the enterprises of Dan Young an Jack Young, if "enterprises" is what ta call'em. An the third is the buildin of the bridge over the Boulder River, about a quarter-mile upstream from the mouth, in order to link up the two sides a Mail Route Road.

I propose we start with Jack an Dan Young. Are ya game, Seedy? I think this old horse has kind a got the bit in his teeth today, even if some of'em are missing. Jest don't jerk too hard when it's time ta stop. I do not like those dentist chairs. They always pinch me right in the wallet. An sometimes that hurts worse'n a toothache.

Ennyway, Jack an Dan Young were father an son, an they moved inta the Town a Boulder more or less at the same time. Around 1930. Somethin like that.

It was Dan who moved in first. He was a friendly fella, always smilin, an he had a beautiful set a teeth. But he was sly, too, an a little slippery.

What got'em up here, as far as I could tell, was the fur business. Foxes. See, there was a fella named Frank Kurth who lived jest north a Jensen, about where 51 an K are now, an he piddled around sellin land an he had some foxes. An Dan Young had a couple pair a foxes, but it was Frank Kurth who kept'em. Now somethin there didn't work out too good. Don't ask me what it was becuz nobody ever told me.

Dan was at that point livin in Wausau, had some kind a factory work, but he bought that corner forty, the southwest one, where the county road an Frostbite Avenue an Mail Route Road all come together. An he put up some fox pens an built a guard fence. An then he built a shack an a little barn, an he had a cow or two. His wife was Helen, an they had a little girl, a lively cuss. Her name was Joan.

I'd say Dan was thirty-five, thirty-six, thirty-seven, somethin like that.

Now the Pa, Old Jack, bought the forty jest south a Dan's. He had another son an a daughter, but they were growed up an gone, so I hardly ever knew them. Jack was a bartender, a booze man, an he got my Pa ta help him build a house. Jack was divorced, probably over sixty, an he soon was runnin a speakeasy outa the house my Pa helped'em build, enuff ta make a livin, I guess.

It was Dan who asked me ta work for'em. Ten dollars a month. That was awful poor pay, but the Depression was startin ta settle in an jobs were hard ta find. So I took it.

I didn't work for'em all that much—a month here, a month there—but I started out feedin the foxes, workin in the garden, milkin the cows, cuttin firewood, all that kind a stuff. Enuff ta keep me busy.

But if there was enny huntin ta do, Dan always took me along. Me'n his little black dog, part spitz an part cocker. We were his drivers. We'd usually go up in the area a what's now the end a Heatstroke Lane—that's before Ed Zastrow or Johnny Rau or Quinten Ament or Harold Brooks lived up there—an that dog'n me make little drives for Dan, an sometimes a deer'd come out an sometimes Dan'd get one. Out a season, a course. Illegal. Nothin unusual about that.

Jack let me use a odd-sized Winchester automatic .22 that ya had ta load by slippin the shells inta the stock. It was a odd little critter, but it shot. An once that dog'n me were makin a drive for Dan an up jumped two little deer an stood there lookin at me. Fifty feet away, maybe. An the dog didn't even see'em. Well, I still had that same old buck fever where the gun would be jumpin around, but I aimed kinda low—figgerin, ya know, that buck fever'd be pullin the gun up higher an higher—an I shot an shot an, by golly, one of'em fell down.

Well, Dan comes over an looks at that little thing an sez, "Why didn't ya shoot a bigger one?" That made me feel real bad cuz that was my first deer. I already felt like he was takin advantage of me, count a all the work I did fer so little pay, an now he was kind a being contemptuous of my little deer. So my feelin toward Dan got a little less friendly.

He also tried ta get me ta take that .22 for a month's pay, but I wouldn't do it. Ten dollars a month wasn't much, but I needed the money more'n I needed that .22.

Wasn't long an I quit'em. But I had nothin ta do, an after a month or so he comes an asks me if I'll work for'em again. So I did. One a the first things I had ta do was butcher a big old horse for fox meat, an I did it right in his backyard. An then I got another job from'em, an this one was not only ten dollars a month, it also included room an board. Well, two jobs, really.

The first of'em was stayin in the guardhouse, in amongst the fox pens. It was a small two-story buildin, an I slept on the second floor, where I cooked moonshine. It took me a whole week ta cook a batch.

Dan showed me how ta do it. He'd sift big sacks a cracked corn, jest usin the heavy stuff, an put the corn in a fifty-gallon barrel, add warm water an yeast, an within a couple a days that whole mess'd start ta work. An that's when I started the cookin. Took about a week.

After the first batch, Dan wanted me ta do it again, an so I did. But I was startin ta feel kinda sour about the whole thing. So I decided I was gonna swipe some a that booze. I found me a pint bottle, filled'er up, an hid it.

Then Jack, Dan's Pa, came over ta see how things were goin. Now Jack was kinda short an stocky, didn't smoke, but he did chew, an he was always hummin a tune or singin. He was kind of a jolly cuss, an he kept tellin me ta "Take a drink! Take a drink!" But I jest didn't like the taste of it, an after Jack left I went an got that pint bottle an dumped the booze back in the barrel.

I think that's when I realized I was jest gettin fed up with Dan an with makin booze. Now Dan started ta get scared a gettin caught, I think, cuz two batches were all I cooked. An then the barrels disappeared.

He'd put that booze in perty little ten-gallon wooden kegs, put one of 'em in his car an go ta Wausau. He'd be gone all day. An when he came back, his car was jest loaded with groceries. Once Helen showed me a brand new leather purse she'd got. Had ta be booze money that bought it cuz I don't know what else it cudda been.

But Dan had also heard that I could use dynamite, an so he bought me half a box a sticks an told me ta go blow stumps. See, southwest a the buildings an the fox pens was a kinda level spot, several acres big, an it was jest infested with big pine stumps. I'd already learned the trade from Tony Zillman, so for two weeks, maybe, that's all I did was blow stumps. Well, Dan hired another guy with a team a horses ta drag broken stumps off the field—if ya could call it a "field"—an I helped that fella with that job, too, for a while.

Now Dan wasn't no wallflower, an it wasn't long an he got elected ta the town board. An I spoze it was by meetin people through the board that he got ta know Leo Gould, who was a state fire warden an also a game warden. An Dan an Leo got ta be friends.

One a the last things I did with Dan was ta go with'em in his old Star car, up past Batchelders'—nobody lived beyond'em at that time—ta shine deer. Dan drove an I held the light. It was darker'n the ace a spades.

An up toward Wolf Crick we saw eyes in the woods, jest at the edge a the road, an it's a deer, an Dan shoots it right outa the window.

Well, a few days later an what's left a that deer is hangin in a little shed by Dan's house an who comes ta supper but Leo Gould. Dan had invited'em. Helen had a fine meal on the table, includin a big platter a venison steaks.

I was jest amazed. But we all sat an ate an nothin was said about what we were eatin. Leo Gould sat there eatin illegal venison off a Dan Young's table, an I could hardly believe my eyes.

But it was good, an I sure as hell ate my share.

Dan didn't live ta be a old man. He was jest in his forties, maybe, an he had stomach problems—cancer, I guess—an he died in the hospital. I went ta see'em, but he never came home again.

Old Henry Rau boarded a while with Helen, after Dan died, an then she married Mark Lemmer, who ended up gettin Jack's place too. An eventually it was Ned an Martha Fox who bought Dan's place, an Ned's oldest boy Eugene eventually married Helen's daughter Joan.

Some a these stories get so twisted ya start ta feel like yer gettin tangled in a bigger an bigger knot a people, an some of 'em ya don't even know. Maybe we're all more neighbors than we think.

Well, let's jest keep ploddin along. You kin take a nap if you want to, Seedy, jest as long as that tape recorder stays awake. I jest hate it when machines start ta snore.

Pa an me heard they were gonna build a bridge acrost the Boulder, jest upstream from the Wisconsin—gonna connect the two ends a Mail Route Road, ya know—an we walked down to the site where the company men were measurin an lookin things over, an Pa asks for a job, an he gets it, an I ask for a job, an I get it.

The only other man from the town that got a job on that bridge was Frank Gleason, who lived on Mail Route Road east a Frostbite Avenue. An, like us, he came walkin through the woods ta ask.

Some people complained that it wasn't fair that two men out a one family had got work, an me only a big kid still livin at home. But by then it was too late. We had the jobs.

It was a perty small crew—three company men an three of us from the Town a Boulder. Pa an Frank Gleason an me. The job lasted a month, six weeks maybe. There was a lot a hand work. Diggin an buildin forms an workin with the iron an the cement.

One evenin, after work, I went up ta Happy Jack's—that's what everybody called Jack Young's speakeasy—an there for the first time I met Joe Smitty. Now Jack had a fish net an it didn't take'em long ta get Joe an me ta go set that net in the Boulder. I was ta come back real early in the mornin ta get Joe an we'd go pull the net.

An I did. I'm knockin on the door an perty soon Jack opens up an I ask'em for Smitty an Jack sez, "I kicked'em out last night." Well, I still had ta go get the net, an I did, mostly suckers an one nice trout, an I brought the net back ta Jack.

Now Jack had wanted Smitty an me ta net some fish cuz he wanted trout. That's all he wanted. I knew that. But I was kinda mad about havin ta deal with the net all by myself, so when Jack asks me "Enny trout?" I lied to'em an said no.

Pa an me had that trout for lunch.

It was a long time before I saw Joe Smitty again.

Well, the youngest a the company men an me were under the bridge, on some kind a rickety scaffolding, takin lumber forms off the bottom, an the company guy accidentally dropped his hammer in the river. The river had been low, but it had jest rained hard an the water had risen, so it was fast an choppy. That fella jest went an got himself another hammer.

But I remembered where he'd dropped it an, when the job was done an the river'd gone down, I went back, went wadin, an I found that hammer. I still got it. It's my Mail Route Road bridge hammer, though maybe I oughta send it back ta the company. Explain to'em where I got it. See if they're still missin it.

Now I'm gonna tell ya about Orin Sommers. See, Orin was the man who cleared what's still called Sommers Field. That's north a the Mail Route bridge by about a half a mile. Orin moved out there with his wife an child an lived in a tent an started ta clear land—a big, flat piece a land between

Mail Route an the Wisconsin River. I don't think that piece a Mail Route was even in there yet.

Orin worked hard. He was jest a average-sized man, not specially big an not specially small, but he was a hard worker. I know I helped'em pull cow beets one fall—they were planted right in with his hay—an he offered ta sell me his slide action Remington .22 for twelve dollars.

Well, I think he was broke, or damn near. Wasn't long an his wife left'em. An then Orin had ta sell his land. Oscar Wangen ended up buyin it.

But I found the twelve dollars an I bought the gun from Orin. After I had it, I discovered I couldn't shoot long rifles in it, only shorts. See, a .22 kin use three lengths a bullets—shorts, longs, an long rifles. The longer the shell the more poost it's got. But Orin apparently had never shot ennything in that gun but shorts, an so that's all that'd work. If I tried ta shoot long rifles in it, they'd get stuck. I'd have ta carry a ramrod ta poke each empty shell outa the chamber by pushing the ramrod down the barrel. That got old.

So I traded the gun ta George Eberhardt for a 1914 torpedo body Model T. Didn't have enny starter, no generator, only magneto lights, but I really liked it, even if the motor was shot. That was my first car.

I still wanted a gun, though. So I bought a single-shot .22 from my sister Nellie. Shot rabbits. It was only a single-shot, but at least I could use long rifles. We ate lots a rabbits.

Well, I forgot ta tell ya somethin. I had earned forty bucks workin on that bridge. But Clara was home, an she had written to some company about how ta get a job with Uncle Sam. Ya needed forty dollars ta go through a correspondence course, so I gave her the money to apply for me. She sent the application and the money an I got lesson after lesson through the mail. I answered all the questions, week after week. I was learnin ta be a railway mail clerk.

After a long time a hearin nothin, I finally got a letter sayin there's ta be an examination for a job in Colorado! Well, I didn't have no money ta get ta Colorado. So all that came ta nothin. My forty bucks a bridge work went right down the river.

I did get a hammer, though. I think you still got it, Seedy, back at yer log house.

I think it's time I told ya about working in the woods for Fred Schulz.

By golly, Seedy, you looked like you were half-asleep, an all of a sudden you're perked up! Sorry if I wrecked yer nap. I don't mean ta interfere with yer beauty rest, but it ain't been too successful so far. I *am* ninety-five years old, ya know, an another fifty years might be too long fer me ta wait fer you ta get fully rested up.

Ennyway, winters usta be a lot colder'n they are now. I remember I was drivin Fred's team, sittin on the haulin sled, an I think this was the first mornin out, headed to the spruce swamp, an I sez ta the man sittin next ta me, "You drive. I can't take it. It's jest too cold. I gotta get off an walk." So I handed him the lines an slid off the sled an walked alongside a Queen, the half-blind skiddin horse that was tied on behind.

I guess I was spozed ta drive the horses an sled from that black spruce swamp, west a Batchelders' by a mile or more, an, following the contour a the land, west a the Boulder, go on down ta the 27 landing an unload the pulp. But I didn't have the clothes for it. I only had a sweater over a shirt, an I wouldn't even a had that sweater cept for the boss lady down at Cranmore, who got it for me when I was rakin cranberries with Victor Batchelder.

So Fred changed his mind an put me ta skiddin behind Queen. Then I was movin all day. I don't know that I was keepin warm, exactly, but at least I wasn't freezin.

There were five of us. There was the man who did the haulin from the edge a the swamp to the landing. Probably three trips a day, about a full cord each load. I can't seem ta remember his name. An then there were three men choppin the spruce. Fred was one a the three, an my Pa was another. Can't remember the name a that third man, either. An then there was me, skiddin with Queen.

I think Pa an me were each paid two dollars a day. I don't know what the other fellas got.

Some a those men stayed in Karban's shack, an the horses were kept in a small barn at Karban's, too. So Pa an me'd get dropped off at home at the end a the day an picked up again in the mornin. We worked all winter.

I think this was the only time I worked in the woods an all the trees got chopped with axes. Nothin was sawed. Pulpwood, eight foot lengths, I spoze. An my job was ta go from one chopper to another, always skiddin away what they had ready ta go, hollerin "Gee!" an "Haw!" ta Queen, an puttin the skidded stuff in some kind a pile for the bobsled man ta load when he came back empty from the landing. Day after day, same old routine. Chop an skid an haul.

We got a break at noon. Fred had a little tarpaper shack by the swamp, with a stove in it, an every day we'd eat some soup that Fred brought. Somebody'd get told, maybe fifteen, twenty minutes before it was time ta eat, ta go build a fire in the stove an heat up the soup.

Once he asked me. I don't know what it was, if it took me longer ta get there, or I couldn't get the fire goin, or what, but when the others tramped into the shack I didn't have the soup hot an Old Fred bawled me out. I jest stood there an cried. "Ah, ya don't have ta bawl about it," Fred sez.

See, I was workin as hard as I could. I was jest a big kid, but I was keepin up with the choppers, gettin the pulp up ta where the bobsled man could get it an load it, an then ta be bawled out like that in front a my Pa an the other men, an not bein able ta talk back or defend myself, well, I jest burst out bawlin.

But a lot a those old Dutchmen were like that, sharp old farts who'd chew the ass right off a kid an then walk away an think nothin of it. I guess that's jest the way they were raised. But not me. I wasn't raised that way, an ta be chewed out like that for no good reason jest didn't sit well.

That winter I put up with it, but the next summer when he bawled me out cuz I was late ta feed the horses, that was too much. That's when I quit'em. It wasn't that I didn't like'em, cuz I did, it's jest that I couldn't take that sharp tongue. I jest could not take it.

Ennyway, we cut an skidded an hauled all winter, an when we'd cleaned out that swamp we went down ta the landing an put the pulp on railroad cars. I drove crosshaul team. But there was somethin I'd noticed in that swamp. On the east side there was a stand a tamarack trees, not real big an not real small. Nice-sized trees. An eventually—I was always pokin around, ya know, lookin things over—I saw that the cuttin a those spruce had allowed the west wind ta get a clear shot at the tamaracks, an the wind had blowed'em all down. With the spruce outa there, the wind'd tipped those tamaracks all ta the east.

Perty soon I'll tell ya more about the tamaracks. Funny how one thing leads to another.

I got a couple more things ta tell ya about when I helped Grampa Coster make hay.

Well, end a the day, him an Gramma'd jest sit an look out the window. Fer them the day was done. But not fer me. I still had ta *do* somethin. So I usta go fer walks.

I discovered that down at the fillin station in the Sixth Ward—I think there's a barber shop there now—they had a radio, an I would jest go listen for a hour or so, an then go back ta Grampa's for the night.

I think that's the first radio I ever heard, though Eberhardts' eventually got one, too, an I'd go an listen with George. Big thrill ta hear a voice come outa a box. Nobody thinks a thing about it now. Funny how something weird becomes "normal."

Sometimes I'd go farther, over those double bridges ta the east, acrost the Wisconsin River, ta look at stuff in Wenzel's hardware store. An what do you imagine I had ta look at?

Guns. Well, they had this stubnosed .22 pistol, fer five dollars, an I jest happened ta have the money. So I bought the gun. Took it down ta Devil's Crick an shot an shot at rocks in the water. Jest .22 shorts, ya know. Little stuff.

I showed it to my Pa when I got home an he told me ta get rid of it. He hated short-barrelled guns, hated pistols. But I kept it an I'd take it with me ta shoot.

I think the only thing I ever shot with it was a rabbit. Lucky shot, maybe. I was gettin a load a hay from the log barn up at the Anderson Homestead, in the winter, drivin Old Jack an pullin the sled with a heap a hay on it, an there's a rabbit by the side a the road. So I sez whoa ta Jack an he stopped an I took a shot an, by golly, I got that rabbit.

Another time I tried shootin a prairie chicken—there were a few around, ya know, after the forest fires had come through—an I could *see* those bullets fallin ta the ground way short a that bird. Those .22 shorts jest didn't have much poost.

One day George Eberhardt came over with a kid from acrost the Wisconsin River. His name was Elmer Swanson, an Elmer was maybe interested in my pistol. He asked if it shoots straight. So I tapped a nail inta the barn wall an stepped back ten, twelve feet an up an shot an, by golly, I hit that nail.

Well, that was all Elmer needed ta see. He gave me two dollars for that gun. An Pa didn't squawk ta me ennymore about that pistol.

I gotta tell ya, too, about goin ta one a those house parties at Mike Stevens' place, over near the cranberry marsh. Mary an Clara an me. We took Old Jack an the buckboard. I tied Jack up outside an we went in an danced.

Time ta go home an where's Jack? Either somebody'd let'em go or he'd got himself loose. Ennyway, he'd gone back ta the barn. So Mary an Clara an me had ta walk. Well over three miles. Jest breakin day when we got home.

We joked about whether Jack got mad cuz nobody asked'em ta dance or would give'em a shot a booze. Wasn't so funny at the end a three miles. Our feet were too sore for ennymore dancin that night. Jack was sleepin in his stall, with his head down. Clara called'em a "hungover stallflower," but we were too tired ta laugh and Jack didn't seem ta pay us enny attention.

5

Our Name Ain't Buckberry

Yer pushin too fast, Seedy. There are some things we gotta think about before we get ta the loggin camps. And I ain't forgot about Gladys Batchelder, either, an how she figgers inta this whole story. Why, she's even got a connection to those tamarack trees, if ya stretch yer mind a little.

See, when I was jest startin ta hunt up in the timber, up in Kinzel's land, an this other guy usta come with me, I'd stop every so offen an look back an look around, an he sez ta me, "Why are ya always stoppin ta look back?" An I sez to'em, "Becuz I don't know where I'm goin, but I'd sure as hell like ta be able ta find my way back home again."

Well, I guess this ain't the same. We ain't lost. But there's some things need ta be looked at before we get so far beyond'em that we'll jest forget about'em. An I think there's maybe a surprise in here for you, too, Seedy. I think there's somethin that might never have been explained to you before. Maybe ya do know about it. I don't know. I can't remember everything.

Ennyway, we got ta go back an take care a Grampa an Gramma Buckberry, an Uncle Hugo, an Aunt Annie. Can't jest forget about'em livin out there on the Dakota prairie. No trees. Land a the potholes. They all got a part ta play. Can't jest forget about'em.

Well, it seems kind a silly ta talk about takin care of 'em now, becuz they're all dead. In fact, Gramma Buckberry died shortly after we came out to the Town a Boulder. It might even a been in '22. Probably not later'n '23. She didn't live long after we left Dawson, ennyway.

I remember her as a real old woman, stooped, bent over, an I always seem ta think of her fixin fried eggs fer Pa an me, whenever we'd been out ta help make hay.

Uncle Hugo's wife Annie took care a Gramma those last weeks before she died. An she was buried in a cemetery near Dawson.

Pa didn't go ta Gramma Buckberry's funeral. I think he didn't have enuff money. That musta bothered him cuz I always felt like he was Gramma's boy the way Uncle Hugo was Grampa's boy. Lots a families are like that. Try, maybe, not ta favor one kid over another, but if ya pay attention it's usually there.

It wasn't long an Grampa sold his place an went ta live with Uncle Hugo an Aunt Annie. Grampa's land had butted up ta land owned by a man named Joe Gokey, an on Gokey's land there was a little lake. Everybody called it Gokey Lake.

Old Gokey had a boy named Gordon, an him an me usta bum around down by that lake. See, Old Gokey catered ta duck hunters, kind a like Old Rhodes did, an Gordon an me'd go down where the hunters had been shootin, an we'd collect empty shotgun shells an stick'em on our fingers the way kids do. Once in a while we'd even find a live shell, an that thrilled us.

So Old Gokey sold out to a group a hunters. An those hunters bought Grampa's place, too. That's when Grampa went ta live with Uncle Hugo an Aunt Annie.

Now Grampa an Gramma had milked two, three cows an sold cream ta the creamery in Dawson. It was Old Man Lewis who had run that creamery, before the train killed'em, an then his boys took it over. Whether Grampa sold those cows or gave'em ta Uncle Hugo an Aunt Annie I do not know.

I do know Grampa an Gramma were frugal an tight. Grampa always used silver money. He didn't like that paper stuff. Once he even gave me a silver dollar, an for a kid that's like bein rich! A whole silver dollar!

See, Grampa was a different sort a man, a very active man, right up ta his death. Him an Pa an Uncle Hugo always talked High German together, an Grampa had been a musician in the Austrian army. Played the violin, an he also had a bass fiddle—one a those big things ya got ta stand up next to ta play.

I remember bein told that when he first came ta North Dakota he'd walk to town once a week ta play with other musicians. But that was over by the time I came along. In fact, I do not remember ever hearin'em play. Not ever.

I do know we were out at their place once, maybe it was for my birthday, I ain't sure, an Pa took me upstairs ta give me a new pair a overalls—I'd never been upstairs before—an there was a violin hanging on the wall an that monster of a bass fiddle leanin in a corner. Pa took a bow an raked it acrost the strings a that bass fiddle a couple a times, sawin back an forth, gettin that big thing ta make some strange sort a gruntin an groanin noises, kinda like a drunk lumberjack wakin up with a blue-ribbon hangover.

Somehow I seem ta recall that my cousin John was spozed ta get that violin an bass fiddle. Or maybe it was my brother John. Cuz Grampa Buckberry's name was John. But, for some reason, those instruments got sold. In fact, I kin remember bein out at Grampa's when two men came out in a Model T Ford touring car an took those instruments away. The bass fiddle took up the whole back seat a that car. Two men by the name a Schindler, father an son, an the son was a really big man.

Grampa's livin with Uncle Hugo an Aunt Annie did not work out. I do not know why. I do know that Grampa sent Pa a thousand dollars two different times. Maybe it was that money that enabled Pa ta buy that wreck of a truck I drove home for'em.

An then Grampa came for a visit. Well, it was kind of a funny deal. He only came for about a week. I don't think Pa was even home. I think he was workin out somewhere. An our shack was full a kids. So Grampa Buckberry stayed in town, in the big brick house, with Grampa an Gramma Coster.

Grampa Coster brought'em out one day an took'em back the same day. What I really remember is that Ma wanted so bad ta do somethin special for Grampa Buckberry. The next mornin after the two Grampas had been out an gone, Ma got a bunch of us kids together, an a hunk a chickenwire, an we went down jest below where the two arms a the

Boulder come together, an we tried ta net some fish. We hadn't ever done that before. It was Ma's idea. An it worked. We made a couple a swipes through that hole an we got a big northern an then we got the biggest trout I ever saw come out a the Boulder. Ma put that trout on her butter scale an it weighed three pounds. It was a beauty.

She harnessed up Old Jack, hooked'em to the buckboard, an drove those two big fish inta Jensen. Well, ya know what I mean. I doubt whether a couple a dead fish would a made a good team ta pull a buckboard inta town. Their legs ain't long enuff, an they can't take the dust.

Ennyway, Ma was real happy cuz she finally had somethin special ta give ta Grampa Buckberry. We didn't get enny fish, but the Grampas did. Well, the Grampas an Gramma Coster, too.

Grampa Buckberry took the train back ta North Dakota an went ta livin again with Uncle Hugo an Aunt Annie. But somethin didn't work out. There was unhappiness in that house, somehow. He was gone about a year an he came back ta Wisconsin, out to the shack, an he lived with us.

Now maybe this was one a those times when Grampa an Gramma Coster were gone ta Ohio, or Kentucky, an maybe that's why Grampa Buckberry didn't live with them. They had a big house. Had lots a room. Has ta be some reason why he stayed with us and not with them. But I was jest a kid, an some a those things didn't sink in. Or I jest forgot about'em. All I know is that Grampa Buckberry lived with us in that old bunkhouse by the river. He slept on a cot in the same room where my brothers John an Bill an me all slept in the same bed. He had long white whiskers, but they were neatly trimmed (not like yer brushpile, Seedy), an he smoked a raw tobacco that'd burn yer gizzard out. I know, cuz I tried. I couldn't take it.

Pa an Grampa always talked German. Ma, I think, could understand some of it, but she never spoke it. An so us kids never learned it, other than a word here'n there—maybe get the drift of somethin now'n then. That's about all. I do know Pa an Grampa had some real set-tos, but it was all argued out in German an I never really knew what they were fussin over.

I spoze I should explain somethin to ya, Seedy. I don't know if you ever thought about why we're called "Buckberry," comin as the name does from Austria. Maybe it never seemed peculiar ta you, cuz there's Russian people got German names, an French people got Polish names, an English people got French names. So there ain't enny reason, maybe, why Austrian people wouldn't have got stuck with a English name.

But our name ain't Buckberry. Well, it is now. Jest like yer "Seedy" now. Ain't no not being Seedy ennymore. Once yer Seedy, yer Seedy for good. Yer stuck with it. So we *are* Buckberry. But it didn't usta be. See, it was *Bachbeer*. But when Grampa an Gramma an Hugo came through Ellis Island—Hugo was jest a baby, I think—Bachbeer got put down as Buckberry. An so we all got stuck with it.

See, Grampa an Pa explained ta me that *Bachbeer* means "creek berry" in German. So Buckberry ain't far off. An Grampa usta joke that maybe us kids, count a all the fish we netted, should a been called *Bachbär*—got those two little dots over one a the letters, whatever that means—an *Bachbär* means "creek bear." He said we were creek bears, the way we went after fish.

Those dots—I think the name for'em is *omlaut*. An I heard that "om" is some sorta sound those long-haired pole sitters in India like ta make. (Did you tell me that, Seedy, or did I read about it in one a yer *National Geographics*?) An "lout"—well, everybody knows what a "lout" is. You can even catch a glimpse of'em in a mirror, if yer not careful.[1]

Ennyway, I guess we were creek bears. Once Ma showed us how ta use a net, we *were* bears in that crick. Though I ain't ever heard a bears usin chickenwire.

About a week before Grampa died, he came out a the room where we slept an he stuck what money he had in Pa's pocket an said, "This is all I've got." He said it in English, an I heard'em say it.

He died right on his cot. It was in the summer. The whole family had been ta one a those house parties, an when we came back Grampa Buckberry had passed. He was dead.

The Schram funeral parlor did the embalmin—it was a furniture store an a funeral parlor all in one place—an they put'em in a coffin an the body was shipped back ta Dawson on the train. He got buried next ta Gramma. An there was jest a cross ta mark the grave.

Sometime later—wasn't long—Pa went through Grampa's papers an he said ta Ma, "I'm sendin all this back ta Hugo." He said it in a way

---

1. Well, something about that didn't seem quite right. So I went to the dictionary. It's *not* "omlout." The German word is *umlaut*, and it has to do with what's called "vowel mutation." I think my father can get a little carried away with making up his own definitions. S. B.

that made ya think he wasn't very happy about what was in those papers. But I never was told what that cudda been.

Wasn't all that much later an Hugo died, too. I don't know what killed'em. As far as I know, he was also buried in Dawson.

After that, Aunt Annie married a guy named Ralph Nather, an they moved ta Missoula, Montana. After that, I don't know what happened to her. Jest kind a got lost an drifted away.

I kin remember a lot a stuff, but I can't remember everything. An lots a things I never even knew.

An there's some things it's better not ta know.

Sorry if I ruffled yer whiskers—ah, I mean yer feathers, Seedy. Well, whiskers, feathers—all about the same.

Jest steer clear a Grampa Buckberry's tobacco, though. That stuff'll stunt yer growth.

Seems as if our calendar, Seedy, is like some comedian's trick accordion. Every time ya open it up there's a different pitcher on the bellows.

Well, I guess ya gotta stick a string a melodies together if yer lookin for a medley. An so I spoze we got us a mess a melodies, or maybe jest a mess. I'm jest glad I don't have ta type up this crap. A lot a this stuff'd never get off a my—what a ya call it?—"floppy disk." I mean the one I got in my head.

Did I ever tell ya about the fella I knew had a floppy disk? He was a double-jointed fella an he—.

I kin tell by the look on yer face, Seedy, that you think I'm makin this one up. Well, maybe I am. Jest gotta test ya once in a while, ta see if yer payin attention or slippin off toward yer favorite nap.

But here's one that'll give ya a lift or fluff up yer pillow.

A man named Charlie Schmidt had a airplane, a open cockpit job, a three-seater, an ya sat in it like three peas in a pod. This might a been a double-wing outfit, but I ain't sure ennymore. Sometime in the summer a '29—cudda been the Fourth a July, I ain't sure a that, either—Charlie was givin rides.

He had his plane on that flat field jest west a Jensen, right near the Wisconsin River where those guys in the waterspider boats usta fish deadheads out a the water. An for a dollar you could get a ride. On Charlie's plane, I mean. Ridin deadheads was free.

I know Clara was there, an she took a ride with somebody. Mighta been Stub Lohff. I ain't sure if she knew Stub yet. But it was George Eberhardt an me went up with Charlie.

Once we were in, Charlie gunned the plane toward town, headin into the air where that gas station jest burned, an he swung kind a up an over the west side a Jensen, acrost the river, made a big loop east an north an west, acrost the river again by the Alexander Dam, then back south ta that field ta land. Ten minutes in the air, if you were lucky.

You couldn't see much lookin ahead, cuz you were sittin kinda deep with only yer head stickin above the body of the plane, an a little windshield in front a each person, an the person ahead blockin yer view. So ya had ta kind a inch up off a yer seat ta look down over the sides. I was scared, alright—that's a long ways down if you fell outa yer chair—but it was—I don't hardly know what ta say—it was outa this world. An I ain't tryin ta be cute.

I mean, ta see things ya think ya know from up there where the geese an hawks an eagles fly, why it jest kind a stuns ya, lookin down on trees an the river an houses an roads an farms, everything is so . . . . Everything is jest so much *where it is*, so neat an tidy, so *put together*. Kind a like a toy world, ya know, but ya know it ain't a toy. Ya know it's the real thing. Only ya never saw it like that before.

Ya know, I never thought about it this way before, but maybe it's like people takin drugs, havin—what a ya call it?—"altered consciousness," maybe. Is that what they mean by "getting high," Seedy? I'm serious. I ain't tryin ta be cute. You don't have ta sit there grinnin at me through yer whiskers.

I mean, it makes ya want ta keep doin it, ya can't get it out a yer mind, but ya can't talk about it, either, cuz talkin about it don't *do* it. It's the *doin* that does it. You keep wantin ta see the world from that special space that ya never saw it from before.

Ya know, it was over fifty years before I ever rode in another airplane, an that's when Birdy got him a job givin flyin lessons, at that little airport, jest outside a Minneapolis. He's the one who took me up. In one a those little planes. An since then I got quite a few rides, an I loved every minute of it.

But, ya know what? I flew out ta Washington state a couple a times after I sold the farm—always tried ta get a window seat—an it jest boggles my mind that there's people sittin by the windows an they're sleepin or readin or got those stupid headphones on, or jest sittin there bein bored.

Bored! How kin ya be *bored* when yer seven miles up over Dawson, North Dakota, or six miles over the Rockies? I jest do not understand. How many centuries people dreamed about flyin, about bein up in the air, an now ya kin *do* it an now ya get *bored*! "Ladies and gentlemen, please close your window shades so we can begin the video."

So "we kin *watch the video*," Seedy! It makes ya feel like yer livin in a flyin nuthouse.

Thinkin a Charlie Schmidt reminds me of the time he was buyin scrap iron, on the east side a Jensen. Wudda been in the first part a the Second World War. (Sorry ta be jumpin around like this, Seedy, but you kin see how it happens. Jest stretch out on the couch a while if yer feelin poorly. I don't mind talkin to the furniture.)

Ennyway, guys with bulldozers usta come lookin for work. Out in the country, I mean. They'd walk their cats right down the road, stop at all the little farms, an ask, "Would ya like a little 'dozin done?"

So I hired one a those guys. He did some work fer me in the pasture, leveled out a couple a acres.

An, while he was workin, one of his tracks broke. Now he must a been anticipatin the break cuz he had a spare in the truck. He rolled the new one off the truck an unhooked the broken one an drove that cat from the broken one right onta the new one, slick as a whistle. An when he was done hookin up the new track he sez ta me, "You kin have the old one." An then he left.

Well, what was I gonna do with a old bulldozer track? Couldn't lift it. Way too heavy. So I thought about it. I got the horses an the wagon, unhitched the horses when I'd got the wagon where I wanted it, blocked the wheels, ran a chain over the wagon front ta back, made myself a slanting slide out a poles on the back side a the wagon, hitched the horses to that track an slid it right up those poles onta the wagon.

Once I had it on, I jest drove the horses ta town an took that track ta Charlie Schmidt's. Scrap iron was bringin a good price those years. Lots a war material ta make. Takes lots a metal ta make a good war.

Well, Charlie had a crane, a hoist, an he jest lifted that track off the wagon an put it where he wanted it. Paid me.

But he wanted ta know how I got that track *on* the wagon. I tried ta tell'em I lifted it by hand, but he knew I was lying. There wasn't a man alive cudda lifted that track off the ground. It kinda gave me a tickled feelin ta leave Charlie standin there scratchin his head.

It wudda been the winter a '28 when I got a sawin job from Charlie Ambrose. I can't remember some a the details ennymore, but my sawin partner was Ed Sayers. An it seems reasonable ta think it was Ed who got me hooked up with Charlie.

See, when I started goin to the Copper School, in the spring a '22, Ed was in the eighth grade an I was in the fourth. So he was about four years older'n me. Ed's brother Howard was in the same grade as me, but later it was Ed an me that got ta be friends. I knew their Pa, too. His name was Clarence.

It was in a shed at the Sayers' place, jest up Mail Route Road, where I'd leave Old Jack when I drove the little kids ta school, when I was in the eighth grade.

I kind a lost track a Ed, but I guess he didn't lose track a me. By the time we started sawin for Charlie, Ed'd already become a lumberjack, had worked for Kinzel, but he was kind of a loner. Didn't seem ta have many friends. But once we started workin together, we became perty good friends. Bunked together. Slept in the same bed. We'd even go places together on weekends, once in a while.

Now Charlie Ambrose was jest a young man himself, though older'n us, an he lived west a the cranberry marsh by two, three miles. Ed an me were only one a the sawin crews workin for'em. An Charlie was workin for the Berndt brothers, an the Berndt brothers were workin for Rib Lake Lumber Company. Gypos workin for gypos, ya know. Everybody tryin ta make a livin. Small fish down at the bottom a the barrel.

So I was Ed's partner, sawin, an we were paid by the month. We got sixty-five dollars, which figgers out to about two an a half dollars a day. Plus room an board.

Now by "room" I mean we stayed in Berndts' loggin camp, west an off a County M. We were expected ta cut eighty ta eighty-five logs a day with a crosscut saw an a couple a axes. That's what was expected of us. We each had a wedge in a back pocket, an since I was the junior a the crew, it was my job ta carry the saw from tree ta tree.

I was sixteen years old.

Charlie'd come around where we were workin, usually about two o'clock in the afternoon, an we'd use a spare saw Charlie carried while he touched up ours. Ed didn't have a high opinion a Charlie's skill with a file, but the saw cut an we sawed logs. Mostly hemlock.

Now there were thirty, forty men in that camp. One bunkhouse an a cook shanty an a barn for the horses an a shed or two. From Monday mornin until Saturday evenin that's where we worked an ate an slept.

I worked an stayed in several camps after that, but they were perty much run the same way. So maybe I gotta tell ya a little about what it was like.

The Bull Cook ruled the roost in the bunkhouse. He had ta get up about four o'clock in the mornin ta start in on his work. Somewhere about six o'clock he'd burst inta the bunkhouse an start ta beller. An as soon as he lit some lamps, everybody got up an started gettin dressed fer the woods.

In the center a the bunkhouse there was a big box stove, maybe four feet long. The stovepipe came up a ways an then it was suspended horizontal by wires until it reached nearly the far end a the bunkhouse before it went up an out. The idea was ta milk every drop a heat out a that fire. There even was a guy with a long white beard up on the roof, an it was his job ta catch the sparks an bring'em back down ta the stove. Nothin was wasted. (You cudda had a job like that, Seedy, if you'd a lived back then. Though I know yer scared a heights.)

Ennyway, it was the Bull Cook's job ta have wood for that stove an ta see it was kept burnin, though sometimes in the middle a the night, if it got real cold, one a the lumberjacks would get up an put a piece or two a wood in the stove. Long pieces. Nearly as long as the stove.

So we got up an got in our woods clothes. Everybody slept in their underwear. An then we went ta the outhouse, which was nothin but a ten, twelve-foot shed that was hardly more'n a roof over a trench, with a pole ta lean yer ass over. The men'd sit right alongside a one another, like a bunch a chickens on a roost. If ya wanted toilet paper ya had ta have yer own. It wasn't provided.

For washin up, there was a set a wash basins against one a the walls in the bunkhouse. A tub a hot water sat on the heater stove. Two or three guys could wash up at a time. Ya dumped yer dirty water in a drain that ran right through the wall. It was all perty basic.

Now by "washing up," I mean ya washed yer hands an maybe yer face. That's all. Ya went home dirty on Saturday night an, if ya took a bath at home, ya come back clean on Monday mornin. Ya sure didn't get a bath at camp unless ya call washin in yer own sweat a "bath." An no change a clothes. I can't remember ever seein ennybody brushin his teeth.

But I got ta tell ya, hard as this may be ta believe, very few men got sick. Well, ya had ta be tough an healthy ta be there, in the first place. An maybe we stunk so bad those germs couldn't stand ta get close to us, besides. I jest don't know. Maybe lumberjacks are jest tougher than germs.

When it was time fer breakfast, we were signalled or told. Ya didn't go inta the cook shanty until ya were told ya could. An ya didn't go in laughin or talkin or go sit wherever ya felt like. Oh, no!

There was very little talkin. Pass me this or pass me that, but that's about all. No stories or jokes or laughin. If ya got loud, a cookee'd come up behind you an tap ya on the shoulder. That meant shut up, keep'er down. An when you were done eatin, ya got up an went out. No visitin.

It was all in one big room, with those big woodburnin cookstoves on one end, an the cookees bustlin about, an a big long trestle table with benches on both sides. An if ya were the new man, ya jest stood by the door until a cookee would come an show ya where ta sit. An that's where ya sat from then on. Nowhere else. There was order, an order was kept.

The food was always plentiful an good. Had ta be. We went ta work at seven in the morning, even in the winter, worked till noon, usually came in fer dinner (though some places brought hot food to the woods at noon), back workin no later than one an didn't quit till five. Men who work like that—sawing, skiddin, rollin logs, loadin sleds or trucks or railroad cars—get *hungry*, an the food had better be good. An lots of it.

A poor cook an the lumberjacks would quit. They'd leave. They wouldn't work at a camp if the eatin was bad.

Lots a meat an potatoes an bread. Bacon an eggs. Nothin too fancy, but it had ta be good an there had ta be lots of it. Pies. Not many cakes, but lots a pies. Most lumberjacks didn't seem ta care much for oatmeal, though, which is a little puzzlin. Jest more flavor in fat, I spoze, in good greasy bacon an eggs. An, a course, bacon then was the real stuff, smoked in real smoke, cut thick, an not dipped in some stupid "liquid smoke" or sliced thinner'n yer fingernail, like it is now.

After supper, the men had about a hour ta kill before the Bull Cook would come in an blow out one a the lamps. That meant ya had about fifteen minutes ta do what ya had ta do before crawling inta yer bunk. Men who were playin cards put'em away. Men who were readin found a quittin place. Some a the men were already snoozing. An there wasn't no talkin or laughin when the lights got blowed out—an, ya know, for all a those men livin like that, there wasn't much profanity. Oh, the teamster would swear at the horses—you could usually figger the more swearin the poorer the teamster—but there wasn't much a that in the bunkhouse. The air'd be blue, but that was from all the smokin.

I always liked a bottom bunk, if I could get one. Cooler down there. Less smoky. Fewer farts ta breathe. Put thirty, forty hard-workin, hard-eatin, unwashed men in a bunkhouse an things got perty ripe sometimes. All that wool clothes hangin up ta dry.

There were lumberjacks, single men mostly, who stayed in camp practically all the time. No family, maybe. No place ta go. I tried it once—stayed on a Sunday—but it jest about bored me ta death. I had ta *do* somethin. I couldn't lay around like that.

I think the hardest thing fer me at Berndts' camp was all the Low German. Ed an Charlie an me were about the only guys that couldn't speak it, an the men were chewin on that Low German *all* the time. Kind a leaves ya out. Hard ta fit in.

After we'd been sawin together about a month, somethin like that, Ed came back on a Monday mornin an his arm was hurt. He'd done somethin to it at home, sawin firewood, but he told me not ta tell. We went ta the woods ta cut, as usual, but then he went inta the office about the middle a the mornin an told'em he'd hurt his arm sawin. See, Berndts had ta carry insurance on the men. Ed ended up in the hospital. The insurance paid the bill. Kinda sneaky a Ed ta do what he did. But I kin understand why he did it.

Well, ennyway, that left me without a partner. So they got me a new one—a young guy, older'n me, but nowhere near the lumberjack that Ed was. I don't think I realized how good Ed was until he was gone, till I had ta work with this new guy. We had trees hung up everywhere, an we couldn't get our eighty logs a day. Ya see, ya not only got ta know how ta pull a saw an swing a axe, ya also got ta know where ta fall yer trees. An if yer droppin trees onto other trees, you spend most a yer time tryin ta get'em down. Lots a time wasted that way. This new guy an me spent lots a time wrestlin with hung-up trees.

Sometime after Christmas, wasn't up ta my birthday yet, somebody came to the bunkhouse, in the mornin, an told me ta go to the office. I had ta see Otto Berndt. He had a big mustache an he sez ta me, "Henry, we didn't know you are only sixteen. Our insurance won't carry you. I'm afraid we've got ta let you go."

Well, I *was* sixteen. But I really think I got fired becuz this new guy'n me weren't makin our quota. We might a been workin for Charlie Ambrose, but it was Otto Berndt who fired me.

Well, here I was fired, but how am I gonna get home? Turns out that Old Man Kortholtz got fired the same day as me. Him an his wife an their flock a kids were still livin in that same house Pa'd rented in February a '22. So I got a ride with him.

Old Man Kortholtz was a swamper, one a those guys who cuts skiddin trails an opens up skidways an that sort a stuff. But he was kind a old an slow an he didn't do much, so they fired him, too. (Maybe this is a poor place—thinkin a Old Man Kortholtz, ya know—ta tell this story, but I heard about a older fella in the Depression who came to a loggin camp an practically begged ta be given a job. "I ain't got ennything for ya," the boss told'em. But the old guy wouldn't quit beggin. He was desperate. So the boss sez to'em, "We already got more men than we need. What makes you think we got enny work here for you?" The old guy looked at'em with pleading all over his face and finally he sez, "Listen, mister, the little I do, you can *always* use another man.")

But in some ways the hardest part a livin in that camp was bein drowned in all that endless slough a Low German. That's what the Berndts talked all the time, an most a the men. It gets ta where ya feel like yer suffocatin, gettin drowned, can't breath. Almost as bad as bunkhouse perfume. Worse, maybe.

But I had no idea that in about ten years I'd marry inta that clan a Low German Dutchmen an be hearing those frogs croakin all the time.

Never did learn ta speak it. Or croak it. Or whatever ya gotta do ta get that kinda noise outa yer throat. Was a mystery to me then. Still is.

Well, my older sisters were workin, too. Mary had a job—didn't last long an she jest quit—workin on a farm jest west a Jensen. She had ta climb up inta the silo an chop frozen silage.

See, a lot a those Dutchman farmers usta hire young people an work the ass right off of 'em. Sort a like what happened ta me when I worked for Fred Schulz.

In fact, when I got mad an left 'em, when he'd bawled me out for bein late ta feed the horses, I told 'em he owed me twenty cents a hour for the work I'd done—twenty cents was the goin wage—an Fred said, "Oh, no! Five ta nine is a farmer's day, an two dollars a day is what yer gettin."

So a farmer's day ain't like other people's day. I kin remember a farmer sayin—that wudda been jest after the Second World War—that he'd jest bought his first tractor, an the guy at the implement store asked if he'd like lights put on that tractor. An the farmer told 'em, "Never had enny lights on my horses. Don't see why I'd need 'em on a tractor."

But he was still thinkin dawn ta dusk. Now farmers have got big lights on their tractors an sometimes if yer drivin home late, specially in the spring a the year, when it's plantin time, ya know, ya might see 'em out there plowin or draggin at ten, eleven o'clock at night. But they're ridin up in those cabbed tractors, sittin on their ass, maybe listenin ta the radio.

When ya worked on a farm when I was a kid, there was no listenin ta the radio, no sittin on yer ass. Lucky if ya had a ass ta sit on.

You could always tell the kids who had got ta workin on farms. They were the ones walkin around with their asses missin.

Ennyway, it was Clara who got me my next job. It didn't take long ta get it, an it wasn't long before I quit.

Clara was a cookee workin under Mrs. Tom Bennett in Tom Bennett's gypo outfit, workin out a Kinzel's Camp 30. Tom needed a man, so Clara lined me up.

Camp 30 was a couple miles northwest a where the Batchelders lived, upstream on the Boulder, on the east side a the river. Or the north side. The river runs crooked there, jest like it plain doesn't care which way it's got ta go. Rivers are like that. Headstrong. Careless. Always keeping to themselves. Jest like a certain retired old farmer I could name. But I ain't gonna.

Seedy, are ya payin attention?

Ennyway, the railroad track ran on the west side a the river, an the Camp 30 landing was jest alongside the track. On the west side. So ya had ta cross the river ta get from camp ta landing, maybe half a mile.

Altogether, Clara worked for Mrs. Bennett several years. Said she liked it—liked the work, liked Mrs. Bennett. See, Tom an his wife had a little room, right off the kitchen in the cook shanty, an Clara had her little room, too.

The rest of us stayed in the bunkhouse. I slept in the same bed with the log scaler—an that scaler didn't work fer Tom, but for whoever it was Tom was sellin logs to—an when I came ta bed the second night, the scaler—he was a elderly man—had stuck a pole right down the middle a the bed, under the mattress. When I asked'em what he'd put that there for, he said, "It's ta keep you on yer side a the bed, Henry."

The men got a big laugh out a that. That long stick was called a Snortin Pole. It wasn't all that common, but it wasn't that unusual, either.

I guess I'd been all over the place in my dreamin, and the scaler had a hard time sleepin. So he had to pertect himself from all my twitchin and jumpin around.

My job was workin on the landing, running suckerline on the jammer. This was a small gypo outfit, so there wasn't enny gasoline or steam engine ta lift the logs. There was a man that drove crosshaul team. I ran suckerline.

We weren't loading on railroad cars. There were loggin trains on the line, but they didn't stop at our landing.

There were two sleds bringin logs into the landing, from where they were cuttin, off ta the northwest, on the other side a the county road. All we did was unload sleds an stack logs for loading onto cars later. All we did was deck'em. The scaler measured every log that came in, an he hit each one with his markin hammer. He knew exactly how many thousand feet were in those stacks.

I was seventeen years old an didn't have decent lumberjack clothes, but the scaler had a little shack with a stove in it, so between loads I could go in an warm up. It was a good job, an I liked it.

Now Tom Bennett was a different sort a man. He worked right along with the men—top-loaded his own sled an drove his own team. He had one a the finest teams a horses I ever saw. He fed'em, an they *pulled*.

But he was also one a the most vulgar men I ever knew. He'd come inta the bunkhouse after supper ta play cards with some a the men, an everything was fine. But in the mornin he was all boss, an cussin an swearin was how he did his bossin.

Workin on the landing meant I was around Tom only when he came in with a sledload a logs. An since I was good at runnin a suckerline, unloadin logs an getting'em up on the stacks, there wasn't enny problem. So everything was goin alright—most of a month—until one a Tom's pals shows up, lookin for a job.

It was one a the Schnur brothers, either Fritz or Ernie. I can't remember which of'em. An Tom put one of'em on my job an put me ta workin suckerline on the jammer loadin sleds in the woods.

With Tom it seemed there were only a few men who'd stay with'em enny length a time. Lots a men comin an goin. Some a that comin an goin seemed ta be pals a his who'd work a while an then go do somethin else. But some a that leavin had ta be the vulgarity, the cursin an the swearin. Lots a men couldn't take it. I heard lots a men swear before an since, but I never heard another man talk like Tom Bennett.

I didn't last more'n a couple a days loadin sleds in the woods. First, I didn't like bein replaced at the landing. Part a that was bein upset for bein pushed out. But I also didn't have good lumberjack clothes, an so, gettin cold, I couldn't go inta the scaler's shack an warm up between loads. Out in the woods there was no place ta get warm. I was cold most a the time. Maybe all the time.

An then I somehow hurt my leg, an that was slowin me down an makin me feel bad. So it ain't long an I didn't do somethin quite right, or maybe I was too slow, an Tom, who's top-loadin his own sled—he was fussy an quick an good—turns an curses an swears at me an I had ta stand there an take it.

Well, I took it an I didn't take it. I mean, I didn't say nothin back to'em, but I decided right then an there I was gonna quit. I wasn't gonna work for a man who cursed me to my face. Not like that. Not for nothing.

End a the day, last sledload, I followed Tom an his team an his heapin load a logs down to the landing, probably three-quarters of a mile to the southeast. The sled road had iced ruts, seven feet apart, an the horses pulled between the ruts. See, Tom an his other driver used sleds with those wide runners. Twelve-foot bunks, front ta back, an Tom put a load on. It cudda been over two thousand feet a logs on that load. It was *big*.

The sled road was laid out through the woods so that it was almost entirely downhill—not a lot, not steep, but always slopin toward the river. But ya had ta cross the county road at a certain point.

Now the county road wasn't plowed, so it wasn't like the horses had ta jerk those loads over dirt or gravel. But when they'd built that road, they'd raised it above the surrounding land by a couple a feet. An so there was one spot that was a hard pull. A short hard pull, but a hard one.

Ya gotta bear in mind the sour mood I'm walkin in—cold, sore leg, jest been cursed up an down an sideways, determined ta quit. But all a that jest kind a got set aside for a couple a minutes.

We came up to within thirty, forty feet a the county road an Tom calls "Whoa." His horses stop an snort an stamp an steam, an Tom jest sits there waitin while his horses ketch their breath. Maybe a minute. An then he starts ta talk to'em. An when he's talkin to'em, he starts tightenin up on the lines.

Now I gotta tell ya something so ya don't misunderstand. A poor teamster drives with slack lines. The horses'll pull, but they'll pull only as much as they want to.

A good teamster drives with a tight line, an if ya didn't know better, you'd swear he was tryin ta rein'em in, hold'em back, even tryin to get'em ta stop.

But that ain't so. Ain't so at all.

Tom talked to those horses way down low. Their heads came up an their ears came back. They tensed up an started ta lean inta the harness. An when he told'em ta "Go!" they jerked that sledload a logs an lit out for the rise.

Now those horses were wearing sharp-shod shoes, an every step was a pullin step. There was no slippin as they lunged ahead. An when those horses reached the rise, leadin up on top a the county road, they were all but layin on their bellies. They were pullin *that* hard. An Tom was pullin on those lines like he was gonna draw the bits right through their mouths. He was talking to'em in a loud, tense voice that was tellin'em they *had* ta pull an tellin'em they *could* pull an telling'em they *would* pull.

An, by god, they *did* pull. They brought that huge sledload a logs right up onta the county road. An Tom called "Whoa!" like he *loved* those horses, an they stopped, sides heavin, an took a wind.

I don't think I'd moved from where I'd been standin. I'm not sure I cudda moved. I'd never seen a man an a team like that. There were tears runnin down my face. I hardly could believe what I'd jest been watchin.[2]

When Tom started up his team again, I followed after. But what I'd seen didn't change my mind. After supper I told'em I was quittin.

A course, he wanted ta know why, but I didn't really tell'em. Hurt leg, poor clothes, maybe, that sort a thing. I couldn't somehow jest say he was a mean, dirty-mouthed, vulgar man an that there was no way I'd stay workin for a man like that. Maybe I was scared ta say it. I was only seventeen.

So he paid me an I walked home that same night, right on down the track, about four, five miles. Once yer done, yer done. Nothin ta do but go home.

It was Clara, I think, who eventually told Mrs. Bennett why I'd quit. An Tom was never friendly ta me again, ever.

But ya know what? It was the strangest thing. Tom'd curse a man up an down an do it at the drop of a hat, or fer no hat at all. But he didn't curse those horses. He *talked* to'em.

---

2. It's both my intention and my practice not to interfere with my father's stories, with his memories, or to add "color" to what's already bright and vivid. But I have to break my vow here to say that his *telling* this story was as gripping as the story itself.

He sat in his kitchen chair, leaning forward. He's a big man, still close to two hundred pounds, not fat, with the shape of his former strength fully evident in his posture. He wore a dark green flannel shirt with black suspenders running up and over his big shoulders, and his wispy white hair was practically standing on end.

In his thick hands, held out in front of him, as if he were driving a team, he grasped imaginary reins. His body was tensed, his face was tensed, as if he were again present as Tom Bennett drove those horses up that rise. His voice started to crack, and tears came into his eyes.

I swear I could almost *see* what he was remembering. Memory, I suddenly realized, is vivid in proportion to how fully a person is really *present* at the event in question. And there was no doubt that my father was *present* when Tom Bennett drove his big team of horses up that rise, pulling that enormous load of logs. S. B.

I think Tom Bennett loved those horses, an I'll be damned if I don't believe those horses knew he loved'em. I never saw horses pull for a man as those horses pulled for Tom Bennett. Not before or since. Not once. Never.

Well, maybe we ought ta lighten up a little.

Actually, thinkin of the train runnin so close ta where Clara was cookee at Tom Bennett's camp, an wonderin why the train didn't at least bring groceries out ta folks from town, I remember somethin that happened ta Pa.

I think this wudda been in the late winter a '22, the same winter we moved into that rented house. I was ten years old.

Pa'd walked ta town on a Saturday, ta get groceries. He'd bought'em an was carryin'em in a cloth sack, an he waited till the train came by, right in Jensen, an he tossed that sack a groceries on a flatcar, a empty logging car.

His intention was ta wait for the caboose an hitch a ride ta the 27 landing. But by the time the caboose came by, the train was goin too fast for'em to hop on. So he stood there an watched that train, an our groceries, disappear down the track.

So he had ta walk home. Eight, nine miles, at least.

A course, the train didn't stop to throw those groceries off at the 27 landing, either. Oh, no! They went all the way up ta Camp 36, which was six, seven miles ta the northwest a 27. In fact, where Camp 36 usta be is now a brushy meadow, if ya kin call it a meadow, jest west a where Boulder Road intersects with Whiskey Bill Road.

See, what's now Boulder Road, cuttin north through all that county forest, usta be the railroad bed. Miles of it.

So, on Sunday, Pa walks up the track ta get the groceries, an he takes me with'em. Ten years old an wearin ankle-high shoes from Dawson, North Dakota. It was one long walk. The snow was up ta yer butt, but, a course, not much on the track cuz the trains were always pushin it off. Took us several hours ta get there. It was past dinnertime when we arrived.

The camp was so big it looked like a town ta me. My eyes bugged out—all that walkin through the woods an all of a sudden here's a loggin-camp town in the middle a nowhere.

I kin remember a big steam engine jest sittin there with smoke puffin outa the smokestack. Steam leakin out here an there. A few men loungin around. See, they had ta keep fire under that boiler all the time. Couldn't let a steam engine freeze up.

I was all eyes.

Didn't take long an Pa located the groceries an, in a little while, we're both in the cook shanty an we're sittin down at the longest table I'd ever seen, sittin down ta eat. The men already had eatin, but there was food left over, an we *ate*.

I kin remember the cookees kind a payin special attention ta me. Guess it was somethin of a novelty ta have a ten year-old kid in camp, one who'd jest walked six, seven miles with his Pa ta pick up a sack a groceries thrown on a log car.

A course, we had ta walk home. I was one tired boy that night, I kin tell ya that.

That was my first meal in a loggin camp, in a cook shanty. But it sure wasn't the last.

I can't remember, exactly, what I did after gettin home from workin at Tom Bennett's camp. I spoze that means it was perty routine. Always firewood ta cut. Maybe somebody needed help loadin cars at the 27 landing. But there wasn't ennything big.

Somethin happened, though, in the early summer a '29. Dorothy Lansbach an Otis Winchester came ta see me, at home.

Now Dorothy was a year or two older'n me, an we'd gone to the Copper School together. We weren't close, but we knew each other. An her boyfriend was Otis Winchester, an Otis Winchester's step-father was a man named Emil Kell.

Emil Kell ran the steam jammer at one a the Rib Lake loggin camps, up off a County M. Rib Lake was a big outfit. Owned lots a land, lots a timber. Jest in that area alone there were three camps—21 an 22 an also Peterson's, though Peterson was a gypo.

Ed Sayers was one a Emil Kell's hookers. An Emil was short a man. An I think it was Ed who told Emil about a man he knew. An that man was me.

Or that *kid*, ya might say. I was still only seventeen years old when Dorothy an Otis came ta tell me about the job.

It was a job I got.

There were seven of us on that jammer crew. Emil Kell ran the jammer. He was the boss. A man named Leo did the top-loadin on the railroad cars. Ed Sayers pulled the right suckerline an I pulled the left. Each of us hookers had a buncher—we were loadin cars from long stacks a logs—but the bunchers kept changin. It was hard work. I think we wore'em out. An then there was Old Man Zortman, who was what was called Bull Cook on the loadin crew. His job was ta cut, sharpen, an set stakes on the railroad cars, an do a bunch a other little jobs. He kept busy.

Leo was quick an good at his job, a young man, married, an a talker. He was always razin Emil about women, an Emil wouldn't say much till Leo'd start in on Emil's daughter—how he was gonna take her out an have a little fun with'er—an then Emil'd start ta cook. An perty soon the blue smoke was goin back and forth between the two of'em, an the rest of us would jest stand there an laugh.

I guess that was our entertainment. But mostly we worked.

Ed Sayers an me got seven an a half cents a thousand. Every thousand feet a logs loaded on a railroad car was worth seven an a half cents to each of us.

Those big stacks a logs were all measured. So there wasn't enny guessin as to amount.

Now seven an a half cents may not sound like much, but Emil Kell was a fast man on the jammer, an Leo was good on top. Ed an me were always on the trot. We'd put out a trainload a logs a day.

We made two, three, four times what the average lumberjack was getting paid. Wages were about forty dollars a month. One month I got a check for one hunnerd an thirty-three dollars an forty-five cents, an that was *after* room an board was taken out. I was rollin in the dough, let me tell you.

But on the very first day, the very first pull, the butt end a the logs were all on Ed's side, which meant his end was heavier'n mine, an so I had ta dig in my heels an go skiddin along ta level out the logs as that hoist went up an over the stakes on the railroad car. I figgered right away they were testin me, ta see if I knew how ta handle the job.

Well, I passed the test, if that's what they were doin, an after that we jest *loaded*. I was one a the crew. I hadn't loaded with steam before, but I'd had lots a trainin on a suckerline, from Old Dave Ament on.

For the first few weeks, I'd walk ta Sayers' early Monday mornin, an Ed an me would go in a car his family owned. Go ta work I mean, park the car, an not come back home till Saturday night.

Well, that didn't work too good for his family, so Ed an me bought a old Ford in Jensen, wouldn't run, real cheap, the engine was froze up, an we pulled it out to his folks' place behind another car. On the way out, that old junker somehow slipped inta high gear on us, jest by accident, an the momentum a bein pulled unfroze the engine.

So we got it ta run real quick. We put the torpedo body a my old Ford onto that new junker's frame, an we drove it ta work. I drove it, so I didn't have ta walk ta Sayers' place every Monday mornin ennymore.

No heater, a course, an no window glass. But we worked outside, all day, all week, so what's a little cold air ta us? I don't think we had license plates on it, either.

When fall came around, an it started ta get perty cold, Ed sez ta me, "You ain't got clothes for this kind a work. You need somethin that's made out a wool."

Well, I did need clothes, ya know, but I was so used ta bein cold I didn't hardly give it much thought. But Ed wouldn't let it be, an he sez, "We're goin ta town ta buy you some lumberjack clothes."

So Emil Kell loaned us his car an Ed an me went into Jensen on a Friday night, right into Livingston's store, an a clerk by name a John Edbar sold me two wool shirts, a pair a wool pants, an two pair a wool longjohns. The bill came to a even twenty-five dollars, but I had the money. I was giving money ta home, but I still had lots, an for the first time in my life I had winter clothes ta keep me warm.

Well, I was makin so much money I decided ta buy a better car, too. This wudda been around Christmas a 1929. See, the stock market might a crashed already, but things were still goin good. Besides, what did I know about the meaning of a stock market crash? Nothin. Might not even a known there was such a thing. Wall Street cudda jest been a street a walls for all I knew.

Ennyway, on a Sunday I went ta Akey's garage, in Jensen. It was open an Akey asked what he could do fer me.

"Got enny used cars fer sale?" I asked'em.

Well, he had one, a '26 four-door Model T sedan—"Owned by some old people" is what Akey told me—an he wanted two hunnerd and nineteen dollars for it.

Well, I wanted that car an I said yes an he asked me how old I was. When I told'em I was seventeen, he sez, "Will yer Pa sign?"

So we got in his Model A an he drove me out an Pa signed. I went back ta town with'em, he got more papers for me ta sign, an he sez, "With the financing, that'll be two hunnerd and fifty-six dollars."

Well, I balked at that, cuz he'd said two hunnerd an nineteen. But he explained ta me that if I was gonna pay on installment—which is what I had ta do—there were financing charges that figgered in. I wanted that car, so I signed. An I drove it home.

Wasn't long, a course, an both Clara an Daisy were drivin that car. Ended up bein kind of a family car. Whoever needed it took it.

But I was earnin enuff ta help out at home an ta make payments on the car. Plus I was puttin a little money away.

Right after the New Year, we'd come ta the bunkhouse after eatin, after a day a loadin, an word goes around that we gotta see the woods superintendent an answer questions about a census. I turned ta Ed an sez, "Ed, I'm gonna get fired."

"Why is that?" he asks.

"Becuz I'm only seventeen," I tell'em.

"What the hell, Henry," he sez. "Tell'em yer twenty-one."

So I did what Ed said. I told'em I was twenty-one. I lied to'em. But I stayed right on workin.

Sometime in the winter, on a Monday mornin, Emil Kell showed up in the loggin camp bunkhouse drunk. He was normally a man a few words, but drunk he was awful loud. The men'd come from eatin breakfast in the cook shanty, waitin for the foreman ta come an roll'em out. When the foreman came, almost all a the men left.

But I didn't go. See, on a Monday mornin it took a good half-hour ta get the steam up on the boiler of the jammer. So there wasn't enny work for me for another thirty minutes or so. With Emil Kell drunk, Old Man Zortman had gone ta stoke the fire.

I also didn't go becuz I liked Emil Kell. So I jest sat on a bench near where Emil was sprawled out on a bunk. I was sittin there when the woods superintendent walked in. Somebody'd told'em about Emil.

Now this wasn't the first time Emil'd showed up drunk. The woods superintendent—his last name was Patrick—was wearin a hat, an he wasted no time climbin all over Emil Kell. Told'em what he thought of'em. Called'em every name there was ta call'em. Told'em ta get up off his ass an get out there an get ta work. An Emil Kell kind a half raises himself up an he sez ta the superintendent, "Loan me yer hat, Pat."

With that, Old Man Patrick stood up straight an looked down at Emil an hollered, "Yer fired!" An he turned an stomped out a the bunkhouse.

Well, that was it fer Emil. He was done. If he'd got up an gone out, chances are Old Patrick wouldn't a fired'em. He was too good a hoister. But Emil jest had ta smart off, an that was that.

So I went an told the crew what'd happened. Old Man Zortman had the steam up by then, an he worked at bein the hoister for us, but he wasn't good at it.

Somewheres around ten o'clock in the morning, a new man came ridin up the track in a gas car. He got out an sez, "I'm Faustus LaLone, an I'm yer new boss."

Faustus LaLone! Never heard of a man with a name like that before. Maybe forty years old. He climbed up in the cab a the jammer, an Old Man Zortman climbed down, an we loaded logs—not quite as fast as when Emil was hoister, but Faustus got better an we got along good.

Wasn't too long after that an Faustus had ta take his gas car down the track ta Rib Lake. Had ta do somethin for the jammer. So we were gonna be shut down a while. Nothing else ta do, so Ed an me asked if we could ride along. An Faustus sez "Sure."

Well, it's cold ridin on a open gas car, lots a miles through the woods an slashings, but we made it to Rib Lake. An while Faustus was doin whatever he had ta do, Ed an me went inta the buildin where the steam power was generated. It was warm in there an jest so clean. Clean an quiet. There was a big arm pumpin a wheel eight or nine feet tall, runnin that entire saw mill. I think we were in awe.

An then, a course, we had ta ride back an go ta work.

Sometime after I was eighteen, it wudda been in the winter a '30, a new fella showed up in camp, in the bunkhouse, an his name was Bob Harris. He was on parole from a reformatory.

Story was that his Pa had worked for Rib Lake, kind of a jack a all trades, an one of his jobs had been hewing ties for the rails. An he'd been hewing one deer season when somebody mistook'em for a deer an shot'em dead. So the woods superintendent took the guy's son in on parole. Feelin sorry for'em, maybe. Tryin ta make up for his Pa gettin killed. Somethin like that.

Well, Bob Harris was a husky fella, somewhere around my age, but he came ta camp dressed in a suit they'd given to'em when he left the reformatory.

I don't think I ever knew what he'd been in for.

Ennyway, he was the new guy, a odd duck, wearin clothes that were out a place in a loggin camp, an ex-con ta boot, so everybody kind a ignored'em. After a couple a evenings a him sittin all alone on a bench with nobody talkin to'em, I sez ta Ed, "That guy's lonely. Nobody'll talk to'em. I'm goin over an visit." An I did.

It ain't long an we're almost pals. An after a few visits, always in the evenin, cuz we got different jobs in the day, he asks if I'm interested in boxing.

Well, I didn't know nothin about boxing, but he's got a set a big boxing mitts an perty soon we put'em on an we're standin there on the bunkhouse floor, lookin at each other over top a our puffed-up fists.

We agreed ta no hittin in the face. An all the men are payin attention. All of a sudden we're the big attraction, the center of attention.

Well, Bob Harris knew somethin about boxing an I knew nothin, an those first couple a times I was sore from my neck to my butt. He jest pounded the hell out a me.

But, ya know, perty soon ya start payin attention, an ya see how he's doin it, how he's slippin those punches in, an it ain't long an yer givin it back to'em. Lotsa blows get deflected off the mitts, but every now an then ya land one where it hurts. I enjoyed it. It was fun.

We boxed every night for about a week, an then all of a sudden the mitts disappeared. I think the office made Bob put'em away.

But by then the ice was broke. I don't know that Bob Harris ever got ta be one a the men, but at least he wasn't sittin on a bench with nobody talkin to'em ennymore.

Bob wanted ta sell his reformatory suit. It was made a rather coarse material. I spoze in part he wanted ta sell it becuz he needed better clothes in the woods an also becuz he didn't like what that suit reminded him of. So I bought it from'em. Six dollars. First suit a dress clothes I ever owned. Prison clothes. Never had another suit till I married yer Ma, Seedy, an so yer that close ta havin yer Pa married in a reformatory suit. One step ahead a the law, maybe.

Which, thinkin a Bob Harris, maybe ain't so funny. Story was he eventually tied up a cop, in Jensen, got away ta Antigo, where somebody shot'em in the head. Didn't kill'em, but it sure couldn't a done him enny good. I did drive'em once ta see his Ma, in Jensen, an he wanted a gun—a pistol, but she wouldn't give it to'em. I kind a liked the guy, but he was somethin of a tough nut.

Ennyway, it was sometime in the spring a '30 an what we hadn't been payin attention to caught up to us an bit us in the butt. The Depression came ta the Rib Lake Lumber Company an, out a the blue, we were told ta pack it up an go home. The camp was shuttin down.

What's a "depression?" What's a "stock market crash?" We didn't know. Was it one step ahead a the law? Or was the law lookin the other way?

All we knew was that we were out a work.

But I had enuff money saved ta keep makin payments on my Model T. I wasn't broke yet.

Ya know, there were a couple other times when I got some warm clothes. One was when the boss lady, at the marsh in Cranmore, got me a new sweater.

An then—maybe this was late in the winter when I'd been skiddin spruce fer Fred Schulz—I caught a mink along the Boulder, the first I ever got, an after the hide was stretched an dried, I took it to a guy in Jensen who ran a little dry goods store, jest east a where the old high school usta be. His name was Hans Harris. He was a Jew, an I don't think he was related ta Bob.

Ennyway, it was a small shop, jest tables with men's clothing folded on'em. I showed'em the mink, an he jest stood there holdin that fur, kinda pettin it, while I went to a table where the men's coats were layin, an I started tryin'em on.

"Do you want a jacket?" he asks. Well, I did, that was obvious, an I kept digging through the pile until I found the one I wanted.

We never talked about money. He never told me what that coat was worth, an I never told'em what I wanted for the mink. All I know is, when I walked out a that store wearing my new coat, Hans Harris was at the door pettin his new mink.

I think we both got what we wanted.

6

Depression Beehive

WELL, THE DEPRESSION SHUT down the Rib Lake Lumber Company in the spring a '30, an so there was nothin ta do but go home, which is what we did. What kind a disease a Depression is we maybe never figgered out, but we soon learned its main symptom, which is ta make yer money disappear.

But it ain't too long, still in the spring a the year, when Faustus LaLone comes ta Ed an me an tells us the sawmill an loggin camp are gonna start up again, an he'd like us ta come back ta work, back to the loading crew.

Well, a course, we're interested. But then he sez the wages are gonna be cut, an we say we'll think about it. Wasn't long an he comes back a second time, still wantin us on his crew. But he sez the wages are gonna be even lower'n he said the first time.

Right then an there we turned'em down. Told'em no.

We were used ta earnin good money, an we were good at the job, even a little proud an cocky, maybe, an so we didn't see enny reason why we should go back ta work an have our pay cut twice before we even got started again. We had no idea what a Depression was, or how long this one'd last.

So we told'em no, we ain't coming. An we didn't go.

Somehow we heard of a outfit north a Minoqua lookin for a loadin crew, so Ed an me went up ta look. We found the place alright, but there were no men in sight an no skidways a logs. So how ya gonna work for ennybody when there ain't nothin there ta do?

We jest came home. It still wasn't summer.

Ain't long an some guy from Tomahawk stopped an talked to Pa an Ma. I wasn't at home. This fella was lookin for some popple logs fer box lumber—lots a towns had a box factory, ya know—an when the folks told me about it, I went ta tell Ed.

Now Ed knew right away about a place off the town line road, about a mile west a where the cranberry marsh is now. There was a spruce swamp an, back behind it, a good stand a big popple. The whole thing'd had some fire damage, but it wasn't bad.

Wasn't long an we found we had ta deal with a agent, a in-between guy, name a H. P. Peterson. I never knew what H. P. stood for, but everybody knew'em as Horse Power. Horse Power Peterson. An Horse Power Peterson set a price. We had ta put up so much money fer stumpage, a deposit ya might say. It was less than two hunnerd dollars, but it was sizeable.

But both Ed an me had saved money while workin at Rib Lake. I had my half a the money, an Ed came up with his. An so we were partners. Only I did all the dealing with H. P. Peterson. Whatever the reason, Ed wouldn't have nothin ta do with Old H.P. So I was the one that had ta sign the contract. An when I reached in my pocket an pulled out the cash—I was jest eighteen years old—H. P. jest sat in his chair an stared at me. You could almost hear'em thinking, "How did this kid get this much money?"

But Ed an me were in business. An we got us a crew. An we got us a truck.

Ed's brother Howard did all the skidding with a team a old plugs their Pa Clarence had. An Clarence did all the haulin with a old Nash truck he found. It'd been a minnow truck—a truck, ya know, fer haulin live minnows ta bait shops—an Clarence put a bunk on the back an rigged up a trailer ta get hooked on behind. All loaded, bunk an trailer, you could haul a cord a wood, if you were lucky.

Pa an me did practically all the sawin. Pa was out a work an so he worked for me.

Imagine that! I'm eighteen years old an my Pa is workin for me!

I think Ed paid Clarence an I paid Pa, an we both paid Howard one dollar a day.

It was jest the five of us, except one day George Eberhardt showed up, drivin a car, an said he needed ta earn some money. So we put'em ta work, by the cord, cuttin spruce. He only lasted a day or so. Truth is, George wasn't used ta workin.

It was late in the summer when we started in on the spruce. Clarence found a buyer right away, at the papermill in Jensen. See, spruce usta be the top wood for makin paper. Spruce an balsam. Popple was jest a junk tree—good, maybe, for box lumber, but that's about all.

We started off gettin about twelve dollars a cord for the spruce. Quite a few a those trees had been fire damaged, but we found that choppin the burnt stuff off, right away, before ya sawed the tree down, was the quickest way a dealin with those burns.

Pa an me cut, Howard skidded, Ed loaded, an Clarence did the hauling. We were all busy.

The papermill paid every load. But it ain't long an they cut the price ta eight or nine dollars a cord. Well, we were still makin money, jest not quite as much.

I forgot ta tell ya though, that before we started hauling, on the very day we're bringin that minnow truck out from town, Ed drivin, I sez to'em, "That's a bad corner comin up. You ought ta slow down." It was right at County M an 64.

Well, Ed didn't slow down, an we got plowed into by a guy from Rib Lake drivin a Model A. Put us in the ditch, cut off two fence posts, an knocked over a highline pole.

We had ta drag that truck ta Sayers' an tear it all apart, right down to the frame, which was bent, an straighten'er out. Howard had got banged up in the crash, so he didn't help much. But Clarence an Ed an Pa an me spent a whole week gettin that minnow truck back up an runnin.

Pa an me worked separate on the spruce. But when we got ta the popple, an it was perty big stuff, we cut together with a crosscut saw. It was early in the winter before we were done with the spruce an gettin started on the popple.

Now the popple was for box lumber, so the smallest log we took had ta be no smaller than nine inches on the little end. Clarence hauled those logs to the closest railroad landing, which was called the Copper landing, maybe a mile northeast a the Copper School. Clarence had a couple a carloads down there—they weren't high stacks, cuz he jest rolled'em off the back a the truck an stacked'em as best he could—before we got a big snowstorm an he couldn't drive into that landing ennymore.

So he started hauling to the 27 landing, not far from our place. Eric Nelson let us stack logs on his land, an everything worked good.

During the winter, on several Sundays, I'd take my model T, with a trailer hooked on behind, an go through Jensen to a farm off the northeast side a town an buy hay for the folks' cows. It was baled hay, wired tied. Heavy brutes. Cost me seventeen dollars a ton.

An one Sunday, in a hurry, I spoze, I was goin too fast around a corner in Jensen an the trailer tipped over in the middle a the street. Hay everywhere. A couple a busted bales. Well, I got the trailer standin up again an reloaded the bales—hardly enny traffic—an the busted ones I jest stuffed into the back a the Model T. So, comin home, I was kind of a travelling haystack. But I made'er.

I had enuff money ta keep makin payments on my Ford, until I had'er licked.

Ennyway, way in the back a that stand a popple, next to the Copper River, we ran acrost a bunch a flying squirrels. Those were the first flyin squirrels I ever saw. Perty little critters. I think we kind a wrecked their home.

When we were done cutting an skiddin an haulin, we had about eight carloads a popple box-lumber sawlogs layin on those two landings. Figger about twenty cords to a car. An then the box company down in Menasha, jest on the north end a Lake Winnebago, tells us it ain't ready to have that wood shipped.

So there we sat.

Well, I'd walk from home ta the 27 landing perty offen ta look at our wood, an one day I caught Bill Jaeger, who was woods superintendent for Brokaw Paper Mill, measuring up our stacks. He didn't say nothin an I didn't ask nothin, but we both knew I caught'em doin it. Right away I figgered somebody'd asked Bill ta see how much wood we got, becuz we still owed stumpage.

That wood jest sat there until the town assessor came ta measure the stacks, an then he gave me the tax bill. Well, I jest sent that bill on down ta Menasha, an it's only a couple a days later I get a letter an it sez, "Get that wood on cars and send it down!"

So we borrowed Charlie Ambrose's jammer an we loaded cars.

I think it was the fall a '31 before the last car was shipped.

An when we got the check, it was for a third less'n we figgered we had comin. So Clarence Sayers an Ed an me drove to Menasha an tried ta see somebody. Well, nobody seemed ta want ta talk to us, till finally after hanging around for a few hours, a guy asks kin we identify our wood.

Well, that's a big joke. Here they got a log yard full a what seems like miles a logs stacked up an we're spozed ta *identify* our wood? But—what else kin we do? —we go walkin along those everlastin piles a logs, lookin, an damned if we don't run acrost a stack a logs that's got our kind a stake wire in it!

See, when loadin cars you got ta wire up yer stakes, an we couldn't get ennything but galvanized, an here we found pieces a that galvanized wire in a stack. Talk about findin a needle in a haystack!

Well, we found it, but so what? What's that prove, other than they got our wood? Nothin.

So that's what that whole trip was for—nothin. Later I thought about it an figgered they'd heard we were cheatin on the stumpage. But I think somebody got the stumpage out a us, ennyway. Seein Bill Jaeger measurin up our stacks on the 27 landing suddenly made sense ta me. We talked like they were cheatin *us*, but I think they figgered we were cheatin *them*.

The only thing we got out a that trip was bananas. We hadn't had enny dinner or supper an we were awful hungry, so we stopped at a grocery store in Menasha. Well, we all were hungry, but we didn't have hardly enny money between us, an there they've got bananas for five cents a pound.

So we dug around an found a couple a coins an bought a quarter's worth a bananas, an that's what Clarence an Ed an me had for supper. Three woods monkeys in Menasha, Wisconsin, eatin a big bunch a tropical bananas fer supper. I think we damn near ate the peelings.

Pa was a Catholic from end ta end, an so was my Grampa Buckberry. An so, even though nobody got much—we were such a big family, an we never had ennything—there was always time set aside for Christmas.

At least there'd be a Christmas tree an a bowl full a nuts an candy on the table. Sometimes that's all there was. We were poor.

I don't believe in enny a that Christmas stuff ennymore. You can't show me ennywhere in the Bible where it sez December twenty-fifth is the day Christ was born. No "Christmas" tree. No Sandy Claus. It's all jest "doctrines a men." That an "stimulating the economy."

Ennyway, I think my sister Mary married Otto Luedtke before the Depression hit. Otto came from a big family, lived in the Sixth Ward a Jensen, poor as rats. An somewhere in there, Clara took up with Clifford Lohff, though everybody called'em Stub.

You couldn't a found two fellas who were more different from each other than Otto an Stub. Otto was a meek, quiet sort a guy. Talked so soft an low you had ta pay close attention jest ta hear what he was sayin. He always did factory work, though when the Depression set in, he was sometimes down to a day or two a week, an him an Mary didn't waste a lot a time startin in on havin kids. Six boys before they were done, though only one of 'em is still alive. That's Glen.

Stub was a husky brute, probably weighed two hunnerd an twenty-five, thirty pounds, an he seemed ta get a kick out a struttin. Cock a the roost, ya know. Thought he was a tough guy. I never did quite trust'em. An he didn't marry Clara till the day, or maybe the day after, their daughter Betty was born. That was Stub.

You remember that old tarpaper chickenhouse used ta sit jest north a the silo, Seedy? About ten by twelve, somethin like that? Well, that chickenhouse started out as a shack in that flat next ta the river, acrost from the gravel pit, at the bottom a Karban Hill, in that spot where the county road camp had their tents set up in the summer a '22. Only that shack wasn't there, then. Otto built it—an I ain't sure ennymore who all helped'em—an that's where him an Mary lived for a while.

Poor as rats. That's what the Depression did ta people.

See, right after they were married, Mary an Otto lived in a couple a rooms at the back a Grampa an Gramma's big brick house in town. Paid a little rent. An then Clara an Stub needed those rooms—Clara was perty well along—an so Otto built that shack.

Wasn't long an Clara an Stub an the new baby had ta move out, too, cuz Grampa an Gramma went back ta Ohio, or Kentucky, ta bail Minnie out a her trouble one more time, an they had ta rent out the whole house to another family jest ta make ends meet.

Otto an Mary an Clara an Stub all lived with the folks for a little while, but by then all a the thirteen kids'd been born—Patricia an Paul were the last two, an they were twins—an so that bunkhouse was full an then some. An everybody, jest like clockwork, got hungry every day, two, three times a day, an everybody wanted somethin ta eat. That's a lot a mouths ta feed. An what are ya gonna do about it?

Otto an me even cut some spruce trees on the west end a that island between the arms a the Boulder—county owns that land now—an we put those logs on a trailer behind my Model T an took'em to the papermill, in Jensen. Only two, three loads. But we swiped'em.

I'm ashamed ta tell ya that, but that's how poor we were, how desperate. We took the spruce ta town an brought groceries back home. Things were that tight.

The folks refused ta go on welfare, an I'm glad they refused. But bein proud doesn't feed yer belly. Pride kin be a real starvation diet. An so ya do what ya got ta do.

But there ya are, I spoze. On the one hand, you got too much pride ta go on welfare or ta ask fer goverment help. On the other hand, yer ashamed a stealin, but ya do it ennyway.

Well, we didn't break inta ennybody's house. We didn't steal ennybody's money. We *worked* fer what we swiped, so maybe it wasn't all that different than spearin fish or trappin weasels or sneakin in the brush after a deer.

But takin those spruce somehow felt different, made ya feel kinda funny, though I don't seem ta be able ta explain why that's so.

Pride versus stealin—it kinda makes ya scratch yer head an wonder if there might be a better way ta be poor.

If you got enny ideas about this stuff, Seedy, I'd like ta hear'em some time. But I ain't got my hearing aids in jest now, so ennything you've got to say is gonna have ta wait.[1]

---

1. My father never did seem to get his hearing aids in, at least as regards this issue; so if I'm going to express "enny ideas" about pride versus stealing, I'll have to do it by shoving a footnote in the door. It seems to me that pride is the "positive" face we put on social embarrassment. That is, we don't want to be seen as accepting public assistance because, at least in part, it implies we are unable to provide for ourselves. But the depression of the '30s, like the stock market collapse of 2008, was triggered by speculative greed—that is, by legal stealing on Wall Street. Millions upon millions of "small" people suffered as a consequence. Pride not only disguises our social embarrassment, it also hides our fear of confronting the *system* of legalized theft. Instead of embracing and

In the summer a '32, we heard there was road work on the south side a Tomahawk, so four of us went up in my Model T. I can't remember who all went, but one of'em was Stub. None of us had a job. But we didn't get ennywhere. "We don't need enny men" is what we were told.

A couple days later, Stub an me went back, jest the two of us, an we were turned down again. A day or so after that I sez ta Ma, "I'm goin back up ta Tomahawk, an I ain't takin ennybody along." An I got a job right away, though I almost let it slip through my fingers.

When I got to the job site, there's a young man standin by the fence, somebody I hadn't seen before. I stopped the Model T an asked'em where the boss was. He was a neat dressed man, kinda slender, no dirt on'em, an he looked at me a while an then he sez, "Maybe I kin help you."

"Well," I sez, "I'd like ta know if there's a job up here." An he sez back ta me, "Kin you drive a loco?"

Well, I'd never driven a loco, wasn't even sure what it was, but Stub Lohff had been a catskinner, drivin a bulldozer, an my first thought was "Stub kin do it."

So I sez to'em, "I know a man that can."

But he sez right back ta me, "I don't want 'a man that can.' I want a man *right now*."

An I didn't know what ta say.

Well, he stands there thinkin, an then he sez, "Kin you drive a shift car?"

When I said I could, he told me where ta park the Model T, had me get in the passenger side a his Model A—it was a '28 or '29 model—an he drove us over to the road camp. When we got out a the car, we went ta see the loco, jest sittin there on the narrow-gauge tracks. He got in the cab an told me ta go up front an crank it, an I did.

Well, that's a hard beast ta crank, but perty soon it run, big an slow—bong, bong, bong—all seven tons of it. An then he sez, "Come up here an stand alongside a me. I'll show ya how ta run it." An he did.

I watched'em shift it—nothin to it but a shifting lever an a Johnson bar—forward an back, that big, slow engine goin pung, pung, pung. An then he sez, "You drive it." An I did.

---

promoting democratic control of the economy, we stick our noses in the air and repudiate government altogether, including its "handouts." Foot in the door or foot in the mouth, that's what I've got to say. S. B.

Ain't all that much ta learn, actually, an perty soon we stop an he gets down an sez, "There's four men comin perty soon, an they know what ta do. They're gonna load rails on the cars. Yer job is ta drive the loco. Jest drive, that's all. They'll tell ya where ya got ta go an when ta stop." An then he left.

So I jest sat there, with that big engine runnin, pung, pung, pung, waitin for the four men ta show. An perty soon they do. Looks like a Pa an three of his kids, ta me.

When I told'em I'd never did this before, the old guy jest sez, "I'm gonna motion with my hands when I want ya ta move. Nothin to it."

Well, that's what we did—loaded steel rails onta cars—but all I did was drive the loco. Took us all day ta get a load, an then we'd go pung, pung, pung back ta camp, an we're jest about back an one a the cars jumps the track.

I figgered I'm gonna get fired, but I walk the rest a the way, meet the fella that hired me, told'em a car was off the track—figgerin that's it—but he jest sez ta me, "Oh, that's alright. Happens all the time. We'll take care a that."

So I stayed that night in camp an drove the loco five days straight, till all the rails were picked up. Stayed in camp all week. End a the last day that young man hands me a check for twenty-three or twenty-four dollars an sez, "That's all there is for now. But let's figger out a way fer me ta get in touch with you, if we need you again." It was the Universal Engineering Company.

Well, I took that check an stopped at a tavern close by an ordered a nickle beer. An I put that check down on the bar. Bartender picks up that check, looks at it, takes a long look at me, goes into a back room an comes back with the change. An then I drove home. Though I didn't waste that nickel beer.

Pa was sittin on a chair in the kitchen—he'd been out a work a long time—an I jest walked in an handed him a twenty dollar bill. He looked at me, he looked at that twenty dollar bill, an he put his head down on his arms an bawled.

When he was done cryin, I took'em ta town, an he bought groceries.

Well, I'm gettin ahead a myself again. Sometimes yer shadow walks in front an sometimes in the back. Sometimes, if it's dark enuff, it jest stays home an rests.

Guess we better let that shadow ketch up, or take a nap, or whatever it wants ta do.

What's yer shadow doin today, Seedy? All rested up for the new Depression? What's that the kids say—"the future ain't what it usta be?" I think that's what everybody's gonna learn—the future ain't what it usta be. We think the Depression is behind us, if we think about it at all; but I believe it's jest circled around ahead of us, and one a these days it's gonna jump outa the woods and scare the crap outa us, jest like it did in the 1930s. Only this time it's gonna be worse becuz we've forgot how ta do stuff for ourselves, forgot how ta *work*.

Ennyway, I think I told ya we were gonna keep Gladys Batchelder waiting, an I think we've kept'er waitin long enuff. Not that there's a lot ta tell. I mean, she *was* my girlfriend, an we'd get busy huggin an kissin, but that's all—we were open about it, kissin right in front a her folks—an her Pa, that's Al, asked if I'd like ta look around that north forty a his. An when I sez "Sure," he takes me on a tour—all cutover land, ya know, brush an small trees, mostly—though, as I remember, he never did show me that swamp right in the middle a the forty. Funny how he forgot ta do that.

I was only nineteen. The year was 1931.

Well, I was interested, but it somehow didn't suit my Pa very good, though Ma was on my side. I was her Little Hobo after all. I don't know what it was that got her ta do it, but she proposed we go ta the bank an see if they'd loan me the money. Maybe she wanted her Little Hobo ta stay put an not go wanderin away. Maybe she was telling Pa again that nobody was gonna be leavin. I don't know.

The price was two hunnerd an fifty dollars for that forty, but all I needed for a down payment was twenty-five.

So we went ta town, Ma an me, an the bank said they'd loan me the money if Ma'd sign too. An she did. Then we had ta go see Frank Kurth, the same man that'd kept Dan Young's foxes, cuz Al Batchelder was only holdin onta that forty by a thread. An Frank Kurth was holdin the other end a that thread.

I got a land contract from Frank. Ma was sittin there with me. That was the first land I ever bought, though it wasn't paid for, yet.

Well, first thing I started ta do was clear a little patch a land. Axe an Grubhoe. You got a forty, ya got ta do somethin with it. Only thing I could think of was ta make a farm, an ta make a farm you got ta have a field, an ta have a field you got ta clear it a brush an stumps an rocks. An that's what I did. Or at least what I started ta do.

Gladys would come over sometimes, usually bring a little brother along with'er, an she'd watch me work, though, a course, I stopped lots a times cuz we were also talkin.

We even talked about gettin married, but I told'er, "We can't get married. I ain't even got a house ta put you in."

Well, we never had words, never got mad at each other, nothin like that, but we jest sort a drifted apart. She started seein a fella from acrost the Wisconsin River an, for a while, he was kind a jealous a me, but I jest laughed about it.

Kind of a funny deal, ya know. It was becuz a her, at least in part, that I was interested in that land, but once I got it, ain't long an we're goin our own ways. Funny how things work out.

Well, wudda been the winter a '31 or '32 that, bummin around, I noticed those tamarack trees all layin down on the east end a that spruce swamp where I'd skidded for Fred Schulz. Those trees weren't real big an they weren't real small, jest about the right size for what I wanted.

Wasn't my land. Not sure if I knew whose it was. Lots a those timber companies bought big hunks a land, cheap, an when they'd cut the trees, they jest let it lay, do nothin with it. Sometimes not even pay taxes on it. I think that's why there's so much county forest land now. Acres an acres a land that the timber companies "forgot" ta pay taxes on.

I guess they forgot about payin taxes, sorta like Al Batchelder forgot ta show me that swamp.

Ennyway, I went in there with a axe an a handman saw an cut a bunch a those fallen tamarack trees into lengths I could handle for a log house. I think it ended up bein sixteen by eighteen. Somethin like that.

Pa had a team a old plugs at home, an I used'em ta pull a bobsled I'd bought from Kinzel for six, seven dollars. Hauled all those logs out a the swamp an brought'em down ta my forty. Well, not logs, exactly. Weren't big enuff for logs. Jest big poles, really.

In the spring a '32, I put up that house. Did it by myself.

Well, I should a told ya that first I'd dug a trench for a foundation. Foot, foot an a half deep. But once I had'er dug, I realized I didn't have enny money ta buy cement, an no prospect a earnin enny, so I jest let that hole sit an leveled out a bunch a big rocks close by an started putting up the log house on those rocks. I never filled in the trench until after the log house was up.

While I was putting up the log house, I noticed lots a times a car go by with a bunch a boards tied on top. Always three, four men in the car. Young guys. Turns out that Stub Lohff knew'em, an he also knew what they were up to.

Like everybody else, they were out a work, too, but bein young an needin somethin ta do, they decided ta build a shack in a balsam thicket way up off the Boulder River, in what was Kinzel's timber. Didn't have enny money ta buy lumber, so they swiped rough-sawn pine boards from Ollhoff's mill, tied'em on top a the car, an took'em up a few at a time. Lots a carryin ta get'em all in where they wanted'em.

They had that shack perty well up when somebody caught'em an kicked'em out. Whoever caught'em also busted in part a the roof, jest ta make sure they wouldn't come back.

Well, Stub told me all about it. An, a course, havin a long nose, I had ta hike up there ta see for myself. What I saw was a lot a good rough lumber goin ta waste. So I got me a hammer an a wreckin bar an went up several times more. I salvaged all the lumber I could an carried it, a few boards at a time, over to the Boulder, which was a couple a hunnerd yards away from that balsam thicket.

An when I had it all on the bank a the river, I used some a the nails an made a raft out a that entire heap a boards, an it was jest big enuff I could ride it down the Boulder, though there were riffles I had ta pull it over. I think if a bird had shit on it, that raft wudda sunk.

Two, three miles a river an I got it down ta the bridge by Batchelders', an I took that raft apart an carried all the boards to the log house—enuff for a floor an the roof. Deadhead raft ya say, Seedy? Deadhead floor an roof, too.

Now I only had the walls raised, so Pa came over ta put rafters up for me—pole rafters, ya know, cuz I didn't have enny sawed two-inch for rafters, or for floor joists, for that matter. But he put the rafters up in a way that they came to a peak in the middle a the roof, which wasn't what I expected, an it ain't long an people started askin me do I live in a beehive. An so that's what the place got called—the "Beehive."

I put tamarack-pole floor joists down an laid the floor, an Pa put a couple a windows in for me, jest six-light barn windows. He made frames out a that deadhead raft lumber.

Logs weren't chinked yet. No stove or stovepipe. But I had me a log house, forty acres a land, an a tiny bit a grubhoed clearing.

I was twenty years old.

I didn't think ta tell ya about the well. These memories ain't got enny dates pasted on'em, an so I got ta think what happened when.

Pa was a water witch—he once witched a well on Grampa Buckberry's land outside a Dawson—an he showed me how ta do it, though some people can't do it at all, an some think it's nothin but a joke.

Different people have different ways a goin about it, but Pa an me always used a crotch a green hazel brush or willow. Holdin onta that crotch, with the wand stickin out in front, an it didn't take me long ta find a vein a water.[2]

Otto Luedtke an me dug that well. After it got deep enuff, where I couldn't throw dirt out a the hole ennymore, we rigged up a windlass sort a deal—a rope an a bucket an a barrel an a crank—an Otto'd pull up the bucket a dirt after I'd filled it. Over twenty feet a well got dug that way. That's a big hole—a *deep* hole—ta be down inside of. I made a wooden

---

2. I have repeatedly watched as my father witched for water. In fact, he located a vein of water for me, in the late 1970s, which was subsequently utilized as a hand-dug well. But there's an earlier story worth telling here. Sometime in the late 1950s, my cousin Charlie Humboldt was staying at the farm. He was younger than Birdy and I but older than our baby brother Jack, whom we called O. O. (Jack is really John, but Jack plus John became J. J., and J. J. became Joe-Joe. But Jack couldn't say Joe-Joe. Or, rather, Joe-Joe came out as O. O. So he got stuck with it. Just part of the Buckberry thing with nicknames, I'm afraid.) Anyway, our father was talking one day about water witching and, since neither Birdy nor I had ever seen it done, he proceeded to cut a stick to his liking, an he started witching, with the subsequent writhing and bobbing of his wand. Birdy tried. Nothing. I tried. Nothing. Charlie, who was eight or nine, had been watching but obviously thought it a big spoof—having fun with the city kid, you know. But he was game when it was his turn, and the look on his face turned instantly from I'm-onto-your-scam sarcasm to total terror as that water-witching stick writhed and bobbed and twisted in his grip. He dropped it like it was a snake, backed away, and stood there shaking. I think Charlie Humboldt became a believer that day. He was a witch and didn't even know it. S. B.

crib ta keep the dirt from cavin in on me. An all that well had for a couple a years was that wooden crib—before I put in cement curbings.

Wood, ya know, is bound ta rot. So it's only a matter a time before yer work might be for nothin. But I got curbings in before the crib rotted or the dirt could fall in.

It was right in that time when I was building the log shack that Clara married Stub. An somewheres in there the Batchelders left for town an the Hahns came out from town an lived in Batchelders' house. They might even a swapped places, I ain't sure.

Ennyway, Hahns had a few chickens, an I spoze they were hungry most a the time. They usta come all the way over ta where I was workin, jest lookin for something ta eat. There were maybe four, five of 'em.

One day Stub was there when the chickens came over, so he grabbed a shotgun an shot a bunch of 'em. That was Stub. I don't remember if we ate 'em. It made me feel bad.

The Universal Engineering Company called me back ta work, late in the summer a '32. Most a what I did was drive a engine that pushed.

See, they were makin a cement road out a U.S. 51. Another engine'd pull a string a cars, loaded, out to the pavin area. But there was a hill that was jest big enuff ta keep that engine from getting over. That's where I came in.

That train would get ahead a me, an I'd come up behind with my engine an push 'em up an over. That's jest about all I did for three, four weeks. Pushed that train. Stayed in camp. Home on the weekends. One time I was bringin the engine back ta camp an it jumped the track. Got two a the wheels off. An this one worried me. Thought I'd get fired for sure.

So I'm standin there, scratchin my head, an I remembered my Grampa Coster talkin about gettin a train back on the track with a train tool called a "frog." An he had told me what a frog looked like, so I went snoopin around the engine for one.

Well, I looked for two of'em, cuz two is what ya need. Two wheels off a the tracks. Two frogs ta put'em back on. But all I could find was one.

There's a kid workin with me, he's my brakeman, an so we go looking in the brush an find a piece a wood that's about the right size, an we make a sort a frog out a that. I told'em ta watch the wheels, after we got the frog an that block a wood in place, an I backed'er up an, by golly, we got'er back on the rails.

The kid must a told somebody cuz it ain't long an I'm walking through the camp an I overhear somebody talkin, an he sez, "He put that engine back on the track with one frog."

That made me feel real proud.

But when that pushin job was done, the boss had me help the man who'd loaded rails the first time I was workin. Only his kids weren't with'em. Maybe they were in school. I don't know.

This time I had ta help'em lift the rails. Each of'em was ten, twelve feet long. Heavy brutes, ya know, but two guys could do it.

Well, the very first rail he grabs almost in the middle an picks it up. I'm hangin onta my end, but he's got almost all the weight, an he barks at me, "Why don't ya lift?"

Soon as that rail's on the car I tell'em, "Get on yer end where you belong when we lift, an then we each got equal weight." An I didn't say it to'em very friendly, cuz his barkin had got my dander up.

Well, we loaded rails all day an I ain't sure we spoke another word to each other the entire time. That evening, after work, the young boss sez ta me, "That's all the work we got for you now, Henry, might a been another day or two, but it seems like you got a hard time gettin along."

I guess my rail partner had been complainin. I thought that was the end a the Universal Engineering Company fer me.

Nothin left ta do but go home.

7

Beaver, Deer, Fish, and Potatoes

It was in the winter a 1932 an '33 that I started ta learn how ta trap beaver. An ya might say I learned it by hearsay.

Stub Lohff was the one who told me about it, an what he knew (or thought he knew) he'd picked up from a trapper by the name a Reuben Carlson, though everybody called'em Coony. Coony Carlson.

Now Coony *was* a trapper, made his livin in hot hides, an so he was always on the lookout for the game warden. An that's why he hired Stub ta drive'em to his trappin area. See, Stub'd leave Coony out, an Coony'd go for a long walk ta look at his traps, but he wouldn't come back ta where Stub'd let'em out. They'd always meet at some pre-arranged place.

Coony was careful, though he always seemed ta walk with a stick, an if ya saw tracks in the snow that had a stick mark by'em, ya knew Coony Carlson had been there.

Well, this is gettin off the track, but this is where those stick marks are leadin me. Coony eventually fell in love with one a Whiskey Bill Sprafky's daughters—Whiskey Bill, ya know, had a shack way up on the headwaters a the Boulder, a shack with a grass roof, the only one a those I ever knew of—an Coony bought a forty near the Sprafkys' an put up a shack of his own. An then he got caught drivin a horse an cart down

Boulder Road with a deer layin in the back, a deer he wasn't spozed ta have. He got pinched. He never did marry that Sprafky girl. An he died kind a young, Coony did, an Harold Brooks got hold a Coony's shack an moved it down ta Heatstroke Lane an lived in it.

Ennyway, Coony told Stub a few things about trappin beaver an Stub told me. An I gave it a try.

First I had ta get me a couple a beaver traps, an I got'em from Ray Trantow. Ray bought hot hides—even showed me a false panel in a wall back of his brother's hardware store where he'd put those hides—an he gave me two traps on credit.

So I took those traps up the Boulder, past where Doc Sievert eventually built his cottage, in that area near Camp 25, an I set those traps according ta what I'd heard from Stub. It ain't long an I ketch a beaver. But it's a little thing, only seven pounds on my Ma's butter scale. With Stub helpin me, I got'er skinned, though we started out doin it wrong. Skinnin a beaver is slow, careful work. You don't want ta poke a hole in the hide, an you got ta cut every bit a the hide away from the body—can't jest pull it free, like ya can with a weasel or a mink.

I only got one dollar for that little hide. But Ray Trantow told me ta keep at it. "You'll get'em if you keep trying," he sez.

So I did keep tryin—on the Boulder, way up Kelly Crick—an I think I got five or six of'em, bigger ones, an Ray paid me four dollars for each hide, an each a those hides meant two or three sacks a groceries for the family.

Not one a those hides was legal, but when yer hungry yer belly doesn't care much about a license or a permit or a game warden. All ya want is somethin ta eat. *Legal* is fer people with full bellies.

I ain't told you about Ed Zastrow. Not that there's all that much ta tell, but him an his wife Bernice an two, three kids were the first ta live up along what's now called Heatstroke Lane. This was in the early days a the Depression when it was a pity ta be alive, even. Things got kind a desperate.

His Pa an Ma had a old house, with a big bump right in the middle a the floor, acrost the Wisconsin River from the mouth a the Boulder. I know his folks had a rowboat that Ed usta pole up an down the river. This was before the Alexander Dam was built, so the river flowed faster, then.

Ed was a fisherman an a trapper an a hunter. I'd say he was ten years older'n me, at least. He had a reputation as kind of a slippery fish, kind a in an out a the shadow of the law. I know fer sure he was the fastest man with a lever-action carbine I ever knew.

See, I hunted with'em a couple a years. Well, I was his driver, sort a like what I'd been for Dan Young.

One time he wounded a small buck, late in the day. It got too late to find it. Next day he got me ta help'em track it. We tracked it all the way down past Eberhardts' to not far back a the Copper School. But it musta heard or smelled us comin, cuz it was gone out of its bed, headed west.

Well, we kept followin the tracks an up jumps a little deer. I never even got my gun ta my shoulder an—smack, smack—Ed's shot'em. So we gutted that little one an kept trackin the buck.

We were jest skirtin the southeast corner a that big swamp at the foot a Sandy Boehner Hill, walkin easy on a little rise, when that buck jumped up in the swamp an once again—smack, smack—that buck went down. Ed hit'em both shots, an I never even got my gun up. Two deer ta drag.

Now Ed already had used a tag on a buck he'd got earlier in the season, though that tag wasn't his. It belonged to my sister Daisy. She'd loaned it to'em.

See, in those days ya bought a license an, along with it, ya got a tag ta put on the deer an a button ya pinned on yer cap. Well, Ed had Daisy's tag an her button, but she couldn't loan'em her license becuz her name was on it. Ed didn't look like enny sort a Daisy, if ya know what I mean.

So Daisy's tag was hangin on that first buck's antler, an Daisy's button was pinned onta Ed Zastrow's cap, when Ed Bosworth an Leo Gould an two other fellas walked inta Ed's yard, figgerin ta pinch'em. Somebody'd squealed on Ed, an so the game wardens came ta pay'em a visit.

But there's the tag, an Ed's got a button on his cap, so they jest grumbled a while an left, never asked ta see Ed's license. If they had, the jig wudda been up fer Ed.

I know, becuz I was standin right there watchin.

Ennyway, that was Ed's first buck. Second buck is the one he shot with me with'em, near Sandy Boehner Hill. Plus that little one. An since I had a license, too, he puts my tag on that second buck, though he kept'em both.

With the little deer, he offers some a the meat to my Ma. She's afraid a the game wardens, but meat is meat, an so a hunk a that little one gets hung inside a hollow pine tree not too far from the bunkhouse. In fact, it was Ed who suggested hanging the meat in there. An Ma sez okay.

Next mornin I go ta cut off a piece an that deer's gone. Jest gone. An right away I figgered it was Ed who'd come an taken it in the night. Who else knew? Nobody.

Another time Warren Schnee an me were hunting north a Frank Gleason's—Warren was then livin on the old Anderson Homestead; Al Briest an his family were gone—an Warren got two deer jest like that, a doe an a fawn. Well, we're cleanin'em an who shows up but Ed Zastrow.

A course those deer were illegal, an we wanted ta keep'em out a sight a while, so Ed sez, "Put'em under that cannon." An right nearby there's this windblown balsam tipped most of the way down—we called all a those tipped trees "cannons"—an, by breakin off a few of the inside branches, we made a nest for those two deer. You could walk right by an not know what's in there. Snug as a bug.

Next mornin, early, Warren an me went back ta take out the deer. The little one hadn't been touched, but the doe's hind quarters were missin an her tail was stuck on her backbone.

Now that had ta have been Ed—even teasin us by stickin the tail on like that—an I wasn't shy about tellin people that Ed swiped those hind quarters.

A little later there's a Christmas party at the Boulder School—enuff people had moved inta the Town a Boulder that they built a second school—an when the party was over Bernice Zastrow cornered me in the hallway an really chewed me out for tellin people that Ed stole that deer. She was all excited, talkin loud, an everybody was gathered round ta enjoy the cat fight, ya know.

So I jest listened till she'd said'er piece an then I told'er, "I still think Ed swiped those hind quarters." Then I walked away. I think everybody but Bernice was gettin a laugh outa that.

That was Ed Zastrow. I liked'em, I really did, but I think he had sticky fingers.

In the winter, we each did some trappin. He trapped up the Boulder, an I trapped down. Each of us had a few weasels an a few mink. An when we had our furs ready, I drove Ed ta town in my Model T.

Now Ed always sold his hides ta Abey Block. But Ray Trantow paid better. So I talked Ed inta comin with me ta see Ray. An he did. Ray wanted ta buy all our furs, but Roosevelt had closed the banks an Ray couldn't pay until the bank opened again.

That was okay with me—I still had a few dollars in my pocket—but it wasn't okay with Ed. His family was out a groceries, an he needed the money. They wanted food.

So we went ta see Abey Block. Well, Abey wanted Ed's hides, too, but he'd only pay a fraction a what Ray Trantow'd pay. An Ed felt like he's got no choice but ta take what Abey's offered until I told'em, "If you'll sell yer furs ta Ray, I'll pay you for'em now an Ray kin pay me when he gets the money."

Well, Ed sez yes ta that right away, an Abey wouldn't have nothin ta do with me after that, except when he once came out to the log house to buy some beaver hides I had. But we ain't up ta that, yet.

So when I took Ed home that day, he had sacks a groceries an he didn't have ta settle for Abey Block's cheap prices.

Might a been that same winter, I ain't sure, an Ed asks me along ice fishing. Only this ain't yer regular ice fishin.

He took me down to the mouth a the Boulder an we cut a perty big hole in the ice—fourteen, sixteen inches acrost. An then we rigged up a little sort a wigwam out a brush an blankets over the hole, an there's jest room enuff inside for each of us ta sit cross-legged opposite each other, with the hole between us.

Dim in there, but perty soon yer eyes begin ta adjust, an there's the bottom a the river, three, four feet down. An Ed's got a homemade lure on a short line—no hooks on it—an he shows me how ta let it down an pull it up, kind a slow an steady, an he's got a fish spear an he's got the business end a that spear restin in the water a that hole.

Ain't too long an a big northern comes ta take a closer look at that lure, but Ed is ready an he spears'em. Takes a while before things calm down again, an then another northern makes the same mistake. Ed got that one, too.

Well, when I told Pa what Ed had done, he wants ta give it a try, too, So, a few days later, we go on down an make the same sort a set-up. Brush an blanket wigwam over a hole in the ice. An somehow I'd got me a lure an I'm jiggin away, slow an steady, an Pa's got the spear ready.

First a muskrat stuck his head up through our ice hole an damn near scared us ta death before he plooped back down an disappeared under the ice. An then, a little while later, I'm jiggin away, a fish jest rolled his big body right inta our ice hole, damn near filled that entire cavity, an I don't think Pa got around ta jabbin until that fish was a half-mile away.

Whatever it was—northern, musky, walleye—that was one huge fish. Jest like Ma couldn't get over that big fish spittin out her hook, when we'd been fishing from Eberhardts' boat, so Pa couldn't get over that huge fish rollin through our ice hole.

I think that fish got bigger every time Pa told about it. By the time he left for Washington state, in '36, that fish was so big I don't think it cudda fit in the Wisconsin River ennymore.

Maybe that's why Pa had ta move. He figgered he had ta take that fish out to the Columbia River, jest so it had some decent room ta breathe in, some room ta turn around. By now that fish must be big as a whale. Even bigger. Might be livin in the Pacific Ocean, for all I know. Could even be one a those—what do ya call'em?—"endangered species."

I wasn't workin in the spring a '33, so I spent most a my time, daylight hours ennyway, up on my forty, either putzin around on the log house, doin somethin, though I didn't have enny money ta buy cement ta do the chinkin, or else I was gettin exercise with a grubhoe in the little clearing I was makin.

I'd picked a spot ta begin where there weren't enny pine stumps, but there were popple trees comin up, three, four inches on the stump, maybe. Not big, but big enuff so ya had ta grub'em out.

I had a stoneboat from somewhere an, with Old Jack, I'd load'er up an make a swing west a the clearing an throw the brush an rocks on a pile. Had me a regular half-moon road, from the north end a the clearing around the west side ta the south, jest by Jack pullin that stoneboat.[1]

Maybe that clearing was a acre. Somethin like that. Never measured it.

---

1. A stoneboat, for those unfamiliar with the term, is not a boat made of stone. It's a flat sled made of planks. Its primary use by farmers was as a conveyance on which rocks too big to lift were rolled and then pulled off the field. The town of Boulder was—and is—amply endowed with such large rocks. S. B.

I also had me a handplow. Sometime early in the spring I'd seen a good used walkin plow at Leek's Hardware Store. He wanted fifteen dollars for it. Well, I didn't have fifteen dollars, but I did have five. Old Man Leek took it as a down payment, an agreed ta hold the plow, but he wouldn't let me have it until it was all paid for.

It was at least a couple a months before I paid'em off, an then I only got the money when I borrowed it from my sister Daisy. See, she was workin on the east side a Jansen, at a place called Farmer's Home. Tavern downstairs an eatin joint upstairs. She was workin in the kitchen. In fact, that's where she met her husband, Jim Meier, cuz he was a bartender in the tavern part.

Well, I had a plow, but you got ta have a team a horses ta pull it, an we didn't have nothin but Old Jack, an he had enuff trouble pullin a stoneboat. So I looked around an—this is one a those places I can't quite remember exactly who it was I made the deal with—I got hold a Dan Young's Model T tractor.

Now maybe I bought it off a Mark Lemmer, after he married Dan's widow, Helen. I jest can't seem ta pull it up where I kin see it. But, ennyway, I got it. I got that goofy tractor.

See, Dan had bought a kit that he used ta convert a ordinary Model T into a tractor. It was one a them morphidite contraptions that people tried, an it worked okay, but it wasn't enny longer a car an it was but a poor tractor. But I bought it. An it worked. Sort of.

So I hooked that walkin plow to the Model T tractor. Daisy drove it, jest kind a creepin along, ya know, even though she drove it in high gear, an I walked along behind, holding the handles a that plow. Back an forth, back an forth, until we got that grubhoed clearing all plowed up. An then we got'er dragged an kind a smoothed out.

But what was I gonna plant? I didn't know. Didn't have hardly enny money fer seed. An then Harry Eberhardt said he'd sell me ten bushel a seed potatoes for three dollars an fifty cents. Thirty-five cents a bushel. Harry had a good root cellar.

I jest happened ta have the three-fifty, so I bought those seed potatoes from Harry. Brought'em all in one load, in the back a my Model T car, an its ass was draggin. Got'em over to the log house—no chinkin, only a door hole—an I spent two days cutting'em, for planting.

Now Harold Brooks was then living in a shack right around the corner from Dan Young's place—this was before Harold moved Coony

Carlson's little house down ta Heatstroke Lane from up on Whiskey Bill Road—an Harold had a gadget you could drag behind a horse an, by goin first one way an then acrost, you could make markin lines in the dirt, so that when you planted you had exact rows, you could cultivate both ways, straight an crossways. An then, when that clearing was all marked, I stuck all ten bushel a potatoes into the new ground with a hand-held potato planter.

Ma an a flock a the younger kids were plantin a big garden, as usual, in that sandy flat near the river, down by the home place. But I didn't help'em plant, an nobody helped me. I guess I was gettin that much more on my own.

Well, I cultivated those potatoes as soon as they came up. I was out there with a hoe as soon as they were big enuff ta hoe an hill. I was jest like a old woman with a bunch a flowers. Those potatoes were my pride an joy. It was already becoming dry in early summer, but I had new ground an those taties were growin.

It was jest into July an there's smoke in the air. News spread fast that there's a fire off ta the northwest, jest south a the standing timber. I always figgered somebody'd set it, jest ta get some work, but I really don't know for sure. Ennyway, Pa got a job quick, but I'd already fought fire a year or so before, an I didn't want ta do it again. It wasn't the kind a work I liked.

So I wrote a card to the Universal Engineering Company. Their office was in Medford. I wasn't exactly too hopeful, count a that fuss with the fella over liftin rails the previous summer. But right back I get a card sayin come ta Lyndon Station on a certain date jest after the Fourth a July, an be there by six a.m.

Cripes! I didn't have enuff money ta get there. So Clara went to one a Stub's uncles an borrowed money fer me ta buy a train ticket. Two-fifty, three dollars, somethin like that. One way. An then I had ta study a map ta even know where Lyndon Station was!

The train left Jensen jest after noon. I walked ta town, no lunch, spent all the money I had on the ticket, got on the train, an left.

It was a slow train, stopped at every cow pasture, ya know, ta see if ennybody wanted a ride. The sun was still up when we got ta New Lisbon. That's where I got off.

Beaver, Deer, Fish, and Potatoes 135

The map said about twenty miles ta Lyndon Station, off ta the southeast, an so I set off walking. I walked all night. Went through Mauston in the middle a the night. A street light or two an a couple a barking dogs. Walk an walk an walk.

Jest barely startin ta break daylight when along comes a truck an stops. Two fellas in it, an one of 'em asks, "Want a ride, Mister?" That's awful good news ta me, so I climb in with'em. But it ain't long—jest a few minutes, really—an I begin seein road buildin stuff, so I sez to'em, "You kin let me out right here." An they did.

Well, that was kind a dumb, cuz I had ta walk a couple more miles before I got into the edge a Lyndon Station. An down in the hollow where the town is, I see a building that looks like what the road office in Tomahawk had looked like, so I start walkin towards it.

I was almost there when a man comes out an it ain't long an we're perty close ta each other. I sort a recognize 'em, an I pull out the card I was sent an hand it to'em. He stops an reads it, an he looks at me an sez, "There's the cook shanty. You go in an tell the cook ta give you somethin ta eat." An then he looks at me more careful like, an he sez, "An tell'em ta find you a bunk, after you eat. You look kind a tired ta me."

Well, I went in an it ain't long an I got a hot meal, an the cook is writin my name in his book, an then somebody takes me to the bunkhouse an sez, "This is yer bunk, Henry."

I think I took off my shoes, but there wasn't time for ennything else but getting close to that pillow. I was one tired man.

Next thing I knew, somebody was shakin me, kind a gentle, an I look up at a nice young man standin there smiling. "Time ta eat," he sez, an I got up.

After supper, another nice young fella took me out ta where the locos were parked, an he sez, "I'm gonna show you what you'll be doing." So we practiced drivin, hookin an unhookin cars, workin out all the hand signals I needed ta know with my brakeman—we called'em "brakees."

Next day—six in the mornin till noon—I went out with that same guy. He rode with me as I drove the loco, with a string a cars hanging on behind, headed out to the paver. A time or two an I'm on my own.

There were three locos, three strings a cars, up ta fifteen cars in a line, an all we did was haul gravel an cement—all of it weighed exactly under the supervision of a state inspector—out to the paver. Load after load. Trip after trip. The brakee did the signalling an threw switches when we went back empty an had ta duck into a passing track ta let a loaded train on by.

The pay—at least my pay—was forty-five cents a hour, six hours a day, six days a week, an a dollar a day was taken out for room an board. There were two crews workin. One from six ta noon, an the other from noon ta six. I only worked in the morning, always drove the loco. An every payday I sent Ma five dollars.

Well, there was nothin in the afternoons fer me ta do but go fer walks. Walk an walk an walk. I think I got ta know every little dog trail there was within five, six miles of the place. One time I was following a little crooked road, jest a dirt track through the woods, no houses ennywhere, an in a low spot up ahead a animal scooted acrost the road an went down some sort a gully. I didn't know what that animal was an, havin nothin better ta do, I followed.

Well, that gully kinda became a ravine, an perty soon I'm inta an area with thirty, forty foot rocks. Holy man! I ain't never seen ennything like this! So I keep a goin, an perty soon here's water, big high rocks, an it dawned on me that this was the upper dells a the Wisconsin River.

So I look around, it's hot, an nobody's there but me, so I took off all my clothes an went for a swim. Jest out there blubberin around, ya know, swimming an floatin an enjoyin the view, when—pung, pung, pung—here comes a ferry boat loaded with people, comin around one a those rock walls. Well, I was nekked as the day I was born, though maybe a bit more furry, an it's too late ta get out a the river, so I do the best I can ta stand straight up in the water an keep, ya know, my private parts out a sight, while that boat goes—pung, pung, pung—around the next set a rocks.

When I got back ta the bunkhouse, I told another young guy about those rocks an the water, an the next afternoon there were four men wanted ta go see what I'd seen, an one of 'em had a car. So we piled in an went. We had one happy time—swimmin, jumpin off a the rocks, hootin and hollerin. I think it was the happiest day a the summer.

That job only lasted till the first a September. I thought I was done, but the boss—that was Frank Pierce—he came an asked me ta stay on, with a couple a other guys, an help clean up. There was a mess a stuff ta do—forms ta pull, pipelines ta disconnect an put away. We worked ten hours a day.

In two months, I'd only managed ta save thirty dollars, but in that last two weeks a cleanup, I saved another thirty. When I left, I had sixty dollars an thirty-five cents in my pocket.

It was a Saturday afternoon when we were done. One a the guys had a car, an he gave me a ride as far as Mauston. From there, I walked ta New Lisbon an went right to the train yard.

I was too tight ta spend three dollars on a ticket. I knew the Valley Division made a train there, in New Lisbon, an that it'd go ta Wausau. I didn't know when, so—it was dark already—I laid in the grass by some old buildings, no supper, an catnapped.

It was the middle a September already, not too comfortable tryin ta sleep in some tufts a dried-out grass, an I kept waking up every so offen.

Somewhere past the middle a the night, a light comes on, bright, in a railroad car. Well, I wanted ta know when that Valley Division train'd get put together, but I didn't want ta scare ennybody, either, so I walked right in the light a that open door an stopped a ways away an called out, "When does the train go north on the Valley Division?"

A man came to the door, peerin out. He spots me an sez, "This car will be goin"—it was a mailcar—"an if you keep track a this car, you'll be on the right train." An then he closed the door.

Well, I went back to my bed a grass an catnapped somemore. Jest the first hint a dawn creepin up in the east an a small engine brought in a car an hooked it to the mailcar. A while later another car gets brought in. A little while later a big engine comes an hooks up.

Oh, oh, I thought, this is it. So I got up an made my bed, ya know, straightened out all a those crooked stems a grass, an fluffed up the rock I'd been usin for a pillow, walked over an climbed up between the front car an the coal tender. I was hardly up there when all of a sudden here's another guy swingin up beside me. An he asks, "Where you goin?"

I told'em I was headed ta Jensen, an he said, "You won't have enny problem gettin ta Wausau. But there they'll kick you off."

Well, New Lisbon ta Wausau, standin on the back of a coal tender, is a long time ta be on yer feet. Can't sit. Jest enuff room fer two men ta stand. Coal smoke rollin back from the engine. An ya don't dare fall asleep cuz if you were ta fall under the wheels, they'd cut you right in half.

After a couple a hours, at some stop, that other fella got off, wished me luck, an I had more room ta move. I even tried getting on top a the coal tender, so I could get off my feet a while, but the smoke was jest too bad up there. I climbed back down.

It must a been ten-thirty, somethin like that, when the train pulled inta Wausau. An I figgered that other guy knew what he was talkin about when he said I'd be kicked off. So I jest got off, dirty as a pet coon, ya know, an went over to the depot ta buy a ticket ta Jensen. Only the depot was closed. Sunday morning. I hadn't thought about that.

Well, the train's scheduled ta leave in ten, fifteen minutes, and I thought about walkin. But I ain't had enny breakfast or supper, hardly enny sleep, an I jest plain didn't have the heart for that long a walk.

I saw the conductor come out a the coach, put down a little stepping stool, an wander away. Well, I thought, the worst he kin do is throw me off, so I step on up into that coach, find a seat in the back corner, an sit down.

Oh! What a beautiful thing it is ta sit down after layin in a bed a grass, standin on the back of a coal tender, an washin yer face in coal smoke!

There's hardly ennybody in the coach, but perty soon the conductor comes in, walkin slow, a big man, checkin tickets. An even though my head's down, I'm watchin'em. He comes over by me an stops. Jest stands there lookin.

I think he sees a Sunday bum, Ma's own Little Hobo, soot an dirt all over his rough workingman's clothes, dirty face, dirty hands, all kind a hunched up like he's tryin ta be invisible. Maybe I cudda been invisible, but fer all that dirt.

"How much ta Jensen?" I ask'em.

"Thirty-five cents," he sez. An he sez it like even the sound a my voice is dirty.

I reach inta my pocket an he lets me drop two coins, a quarter an a dime, inta his hand. An he walks away an sez not one single simple word.

I don't know if he washed that money before he turned it in or if he took it to the dump or threw it out the window.

Ennyway, that train pulled inta Jensen about twelve, twelve-thirty. I still had over a mile ta walk ta get ta Grampa an Gramma's.

When I knocked on the door, an Gramma comes ta open it, she hollers, "Oh, my God! I think it's Henry, but I ain't even sure!" An she pushes me back inta the yard an brings me out a big tub a hot water, soap, an a towel.

Well, I'm down ta my undershirt, latherin an scrubbing an blubberin in that tub a hot water, an Grampa Coster—he's sittin on the stoop watchin me, while Gramma's makin me somethin ta eat—he sez, "You got ta fix up yer log shack, Henry, cuz Gramma an me are gonna come live with you this winter."

You cudda knocked me over with a feather. I jest turned an looked at'em—soot all over my hair an clothes an shoes, soapy lather all over my face an arms—an I opened my mouth ta say something, or ask something, but no words came out. Nothin. Not a single simple word.

Grampa jest sat there lookin at me. I think he must a seen a Sunday bum, his oldest daughter's own Little Hobo, but I didn't know how ta even ask'em that.

You cudda knocked me over with a feather.

A Reflective Afterword to Volume One of Henry Buckberry's Stories

by C. D. Buckberry

I KNEW MY FATHER'S stories were interesting, and I knew he liked to tell them. But I had no idea he would stride to center stage and begin to *perform* with unabashed self-confidence and self-assured poise. The project I thought *I* was directing turned instantly into something for which I was a mere technical consultant, a word janitor, the guy who got to sweep up the discard commas and periods, who was maybe entrusted with the job of turning out the lights. My vanity, in other words, got a swift kick in the pants. Glib condescension was transformed into stunned astonishment—with a prickly thread of aggravation thrown in with which to floss my toothless gums. There were moments I would've bit Henry if I'd had any teeth. Envy. Jealousy. Call it what you will. It's hard to let go of lofty expectations, especially after I'd cast myself as the Creative Enabler. Nothing hurts like cultivated smugness run over by natural talent. Ouch and goddamit.

Howsomeever, I'm going to get down on my hands and knees and begin to pick up the sharp slivers and scattered shards of my shattered pride, glue them together as best as I can, and get to work on volume two.

It's too late to run away and hide, although I'd like to. Plus, I'm thinking about asking my cousin Efrazima—she lives in Oregon now—to write a nice little Introduction for the next book.

I remember Efie from our first family trip to Washington, by train, in the early 1950s. She had long, thick pigtails, and she seemed to find my crewcut oddly amusing. But I kind of liked her. Sort of. I *knew* she liked my father. She was on his lap at every possible moment. And he, with no daughter, was obviously tickled pink by her dreamy attention and snuggly affection. (Well, I was a *little* jealous, although I didn't mean to knot her pigtails *so* tightly that it took her Mom nearly three hours to get them undone. I suppose I should've said I was sorry. Except that I wasn't, really. Couldn't tell a lie, and all that. My father gave me a dandy lickin.)

Anyway, Henry Buckberry is not exactly nagging me to get on with this project. He doesn't have to nag. In fact, he needn't say a word. Unfortunately, I can read his mood just by walking into his presence. He's got stories climbing out of his pockets and sliding off his nose. You can actually *feel* the squirmy little buggers. Disgusting.

Well, to hell with my blistered pride. We might as well get back to work. I'll write to Efie later. I just hope she writes something nice and leaves out the part about the lickin.

www.ingramcontent.com/pod-product-compliance
Lightning Source LLC
Chambersburg PA
CBHW071435160426
43195CB00013B/1913